ADVANCE PRAISE

"Finally! A self-help book that keeps the reader engaged from start to finish! Dr. Castro's novel approach of weaving such captivating and applicable vignettes all the way through his easy-to-understand life lessons is both informative and entertaining. Read this book, and your life will improve by learning the secret of giving room."

—**Kelly Perdew**, CEO of RotoHog.com,
winner of season 2 of *The Apprentice*,
and author of *Take Command: 10 Leadership Principles
I Learned in the Military and Put to Work for Donald Trump*

"Dr. Castro's fresh approach to storytelling to illuminate his personal growth message is captivating. I highly recommend this book to all who are feeling squeezed by life and just want to break out of the 'rat race.'"

—**Ricky Paull Goldin**, actor, *The Guiding Light*

"Dr. Castro candidly discusses his own childhood, marriage, and career, as well as the problems he has helped patients work on in therapy. He offers several principles—organized around the theme of 'giving room'—that readers can use to understand and improve their lives and relationships. Many parents should find this book to be especially interesting and helpful."

—**Scott R. Harris**, associate professor of sociology,
Saint Louis University,
and author of *The Meanings of Marital Equality*

"Dr. Castro's book is lively, with many anecdotes, vignettes, and stories. The psychological concepts and therapy issues are well portrayed. Dr. Castro gives a personal, inside, and informed view of psychotherapy (a complex and often misunderstood human, and humane, experience). *Creating Space for Happiness* deserves to be widely read."

—**Dr. Duane Hagen**, chair emeritus,
Department of Psychiatry, St. John's Mercy Health Care;
clinical professor of psychiatry, St. Louis University;
and coauthor of *Job Loss: A Psychiatric Perspective*

"Dr. Castro presents a sound and practical approach for coping with personal life experiences that can stunt our ability to grow. *Creating Space for Happiness* shows us ways to give ourselves room to grow. It is one of those rare books that can give us power to transform lives and even save them."

—**Ed Garcia, MD**, chairman, Department of Psychiatry,
St. John's Mercy Medical Center

"*Creating Space for Happiness* is a refreshing look into the life and work of a respected psychologist who is working at living the loving/free-spirited/disciplined life that he is helping his clients regain. This is a brilliant work that teaches people some key elements that make life more fulfilling and stress-free."

—**Darek Laviolette**, Special Operations Chief,
US Navy SEAL

"Even being a psychologist for seventeen years, I found ideas in this book that I now put to use in my work and in my daily life. Whether I am reminding myself that it is good for my son to be frustrated a bit as he learns or I am catching myself assuming I know how a client feels, I create space in myself and my actions to wait and learn. I know that waiting and learning are on the path to happiness."

—**Dr. Rick Scott**, psychologist

creating space for

HAPPINESS

Dr. Anthony J. Castro

creating space for

HAPPINESS

the secret of

GIVING
ROOM

Prometheus Books

59 John Glenn Drive
Amherst, New York 14228–2119

Published 2009 by Prometheus Books

Inquiries should be addressed to
Prometheus Books
59 John Glenn Drive
Amherst, New York 14228–2119
VOICE: 716–691–0133, ext. 210
FAX: 716–691–0137
WWW.PROMETHEUSBOOKS.COM

13 12 11 10 09   5 4 3 2 1

Library of Congress Cataloging-in-Publication Data

Castro, Anthony J., 1971–
   Creating space for happiness : the secret of giving room / Anthony J. Castro.
      p. cm.
   ISBN 978–1–59102–668–6 (pbk.)
   1. Personal space—Psychological aspects. 2. Adaptability (Psychology)
3. Maturation (Psychology) 4. Happiness. 5. Castro, Anthony J., 1971– I. Title.
BF697.C286 2008
158—dc22

                                                    2008032745

Printed in the United States of America on acid-free paper

To my cousin Robby.
Thank you for caring enough to speak your mind.
I miss you.

CONTENTS

CONTENTS

CONTENTS

ACKNOWLEDGMENTS

I extend my deepest gratitude and endless admiration to the following individuals who "got their hands dirty" by giving their time and minds to this book. Steve Sergi, for his edits and encouragement to "write on!" after sending him the first thirty pages. Jo-Ann Langseth, for her professional editing. I knew you were the right person for the job when you e-mailed me, "You should hire me because I've been having a love affair with the English language for thirty-five years!" Dr. Rick Scott, for his impeccable attention to detail, and his wife, Lisa, for her constructive suggestions always framed in the positive. Dr. Craig Rodgers, for writing the foreword. You are brilliant and unique; two wonderful qualities, my friend! And finally, thank you, Steven L. Mitchell and the entire acquisitions department at Prometheus Books, for believing in my words.

Immense thanks to my family, friends, and colleagues

ACKNOWLEDGMENTS

whose enthusiasm shined on this project. To name a few: Scott Byrnes, Jeff Kline, Scott Harris, Stephanie Stanley, Joel Koenig, Duane Hagan, Darek Laviolette, Kelly Perdew, Ricky Paull Goldin, Andrea Dent, Marc Braun, Felicia Carroll, Judy Blives, Fest Boys, Bill Bumberry, Ed Garcia, Elliot Chapel Community, Mindy McCoy, Deb Gibson, and Katie Ventura. Thanks to my parents and siblings for their unconditional love and spunky Italian spirit. And to my supportive and caring wife, Missy. Thank you for believing in me when many didn't.

Further, I want my patients to know how much I appreciate all of you. It is such a rewarding profession to help others. Yet, the bonus is that every day your willingness to Give Room for change ignites my personal courage to grow.

Last, thank you to Holly for making this book possible.

FOREWORD

by Dr. Craig Rodgers

The word *happiness* is derived from the thirteenth-century Old Norse word *hap*, which means "a chance or luck occurrence." Thus, our question—or perhaps, our quest—can be framed as "If happiness is a game of chance, then how might I increase my odds of winning?"

Variations of this question are as old as humankind itself. Answers to this question are equally ancient. Throughout history, individuals and institutions have proffered countless responses to this question of how to find or achieve happiness—responses that are culturally, religiously, scientifically, and civically based. These various paths to happiness might involve, for example, adhering to a set of beliefs or behaviors, or taking psychotropic medications, or plumbing the depths of one's own psyche.

Regardless of how one chooses to pursue happiness, the

quest is dynamic, not static. It requires a *change* in some combination of one's feeling, thinking, or behavior. And change requires *effort*, which in today's world might involve varying degrees of gentle nurturing, diligent maintenance, openness, acceptance, and resiliency. In *Creating Space for Happiness: The Secret of Giving Room*, Dr. Castro demystifies and detoxifies the effort. By communicating in his characteristically warm, informal style and by drawing upon autobiographical anecdotes as well as his professional experiences as a therapist, Dr. Castro both educates and entertains the reader as he describes what it means to "create space" and "give room."

To make use of a "self-help" text, that text must first and foremost resonate with the reader. It must successfully balance specificity with universal appeal and it must touch upon themes in a way that will allow readers to weave their individual threads into a uniquely personal, meaningful tapestry. In *Creating Space for Happiness*, Dr. Castro delves into the familiar territory of perfectionism, motivation, guilt, conflict, and compromise. Dr. Castro covers these themes from developmental vantage points throughout the life span, for example, as child, as adolescent, as partner, as parent, as friend. By viewing the pursuit of happiness through these multiple lenses, the reader is far better equipped to synthesize, integrate, and apply the lessons than if those lessons had been presented from a more myopic, singular perspective.

When I finished reading *Creating Space for Happiness* and reflected upon what I had learned, the image of a campfire came to mind. A campfire will not start easily, if at all, when wet leaves or green wood is involved. Rather, the conditions need to be decent enough—not necessarily *perfect*, mind you, but just decent enough—to allow a largely static, slowly decaying pile of kindling and tinder to morph slowly and steadily into the crackling, roaring blaze that envelops those around it with warmth, comfort, and security.

Controlled human intervention allows us to physically transform the inert detritus on the forest floor into the glowing embers of our fire that at times can mean the difference between life and death. Similarly, achieving and maintaining happiness involves the *mental* conversion and interpretation of one's otherwise routine, mundane, day-to-day experiences in a manner that leaves us, and often those we care about, feeling better and more alive. As this book emphasizes by its consistent focus on ordinary people, this conversion and interpretation has nothing to do with fame, money, or privilege.

Through his book, Dr. Castro will show you how to build that campfire from start to finish and how to empower you to build your own fires whenever you need their warmth in the future. He will show you how to select the best tinder and kindling. He will show you how to arrange it most effectively. He will show you how to light your fire, how to grow it, and how to maintain it. And perhaps most importantly, Dr. Castro will show you how to appreciate and enjoy it.

Enjoy the adventure, be well, and stay warm!

PREFACE

During my years in graduate school, professors would frequently tell me that I was much better at telling stories than writing technical papers. Over and over again, my research papers would receive less favorable grades than those of my graduate school colleagues. When I would ask my professors about their views of my work, they would make comments like "Mr. Castro, it was a great paper if you were submitting it to the *New Yorker*, but this is a doctoral program in clinical psychology, and it's time you started writing in that manner."

I never did change my style of writing. True to form, this book is written in my informal style and contains many stories. I hope that while you're reading this book, you will feel that we're having a conversation rather than feeling as though I'm lecturing you on an array of psychological concepts.

PREFACE

In the tradition of offering practical, helpful tools through storytelling, I will also be weaving a short story throughout the book. This story is about a child named Holly. It involves several different people whom I've met through my work and includes events from their lives. These are REAL people, but, of course, I have been diligent to change their names and disguise the particulars to protect the confidentiality of those involved. But the themes, messages, and lessons all remain untouched. Holly's story, and all the other stories you'll be reading in this book, help illustrate the personal growth principles I discuss throughout.

I have yet to meet a human being who doesn't have issues. Everyone has issues! Everyone has baggage, even if many of us find it hard to remember in our adult lives. It doesn't matter if you have come from money or grew up poverty-stricken. Issues don't hide from gender or race, from the old or young, or from the rich or poor. People who are physically healthy and fit have their issues just like the ten-year-old girl who has been suffering from cancer for the past five years and has now started to comprehend that it is unlikely she will ever reach her teenage years.

And yes, this successful practicing psychologist, who grew up in affluence and is now living in predominantly white upper-class suburbia in one of the most racially divided cities in America, has got some issues and baggage too. I want the reader to know this right from the beginning. You see, life is all about baggage and how you deal with it. And frankly, the goal of this book is to free you up by helping you find room to store—and maybe even lose—some of that baggage. Traveling more lightly, you may find it easier to find the space in your life—space in which you will ultimately Give Room for happiness.

GIVING ROOM

began my quest to write this book several years ago. The process went like this: Something powerfully enlightening would emerge during a psychotherapy session I was conducting. For instance, words from the patient or perhaps from me would trigger an "A ha!" moment for *both* of us, sending a wave of insight and personal growth that would flood the room. Or this moment might be more subtle, the words not as important as the nonverbal flow and exchange during the therapeutic hour. Either way, as a result of that "A ha!" moment, both patient and therapist gained new insight.

In addition to my work as a therapist, personal life lessons fueled me to write this book. These life lessons, along with the insights gained during my therapeutic work, would also fall under step one of creating this book. Whether I was the therapist, partner, friend, brother, or dad, striking human interactions would come up in my life over and over, and the neurons in my brain would start firing. I would then turn on my computer and open the file I had titled *Giving Room*. This led to step two: I began furiously typing up the event or situation, personal or professional, that caught my attention. I wanted to try to somehow use these new insights as springboards to improving others' lives.

After reviewing several pages of these thoughts, I finally took the plunge and heard myself pronounce those immortal words: "I'm going to write this book!" I would arrive at my office in the wee hours of the morning and, before seeing my first patient, I would muddle along for hours, trying to turn many of the jumbled profundities in the *Giving Room* file into coherent thoughts. Fast-forward to the present and voila! The book is done, and I am happy with it.

I had two goals when I began, and I believe both will be achieved. First, I wanted the book to be helpful. "Wow, I can really use that idea or concept in my everyday life!" would be music to my ears. Second, I wanted the book to be entertaining. I hoped that you would be left saying, "That was a lot of fun to read!"

Upon completion, however, the manuscript had one problem. I realized I had never given a specific definition of *Giving Room*. I was certain it did have meaning; I was just confused about how to describe it. Nevertheless, I had an understanding that Giving Room was much larger than the sum of its parts. Kind of like a Tastykake, whose slogan is *all the good things wrapped up in one*! Professional authors, talented colleagues, bright friends, they all read the book and loved it. Yet when I asked, "So how would you define this phrase, *Giving Room*?" that deer-in-the-headlights look would appear on their faces. They *felt* what Giving Room was all about, but still my friends and colleagues would stumble over their words: "Well, you know, Anthony. It's about, um, you know. Giving Room is, uhh . . ." I quickly learned to bail them out by commenting, "Ah, forget it. The good news is that you liked the book."

Before reading the book, my psychologist buddy Rick Scott interpreted the title *Giving Room* as a place, not an action. In other words, he assumed he would be reading a book about what happened in my office: The Giving Room! I suppose my office is a Giving Room, but as you will soon discover, my intent is to create an understanding that Giving Room is an action. It is a verb, not a noun, implying movement. Of this, I was certain.

I must admit that I hadn't read my book from start to finish until recently. Once I did, my understanding of this Zen-like phrase, Giving Room, began to surface in my consciousness. Giving Room requires giving yourself space and having a willingness to put energy into something with no guarantees. Giving Room allows you to "sit" with a situation, an emotion, a reaction—anything—and give yourself time to reflect and to allow a natural, organic process to take place. Giving Room keeps you from reacting "from your gut" and necessitates a more thoughtful response.

Giving Room is also a matter of perspective. Whether you have a yearning deep in your gut to improve yourself as a parent, a partner, or a person, remember, Giving Room is about taking a deep breath and "suffering for your own good." By this, I mean doing something different than what you're used to, which can be difficult for many of us. For me personally, Giving Room was about giving myself permission to write this book for you. Understand, this book doesn't have life lessons neatly displayed with bullet points like most self-help books. Certainly, I give concrete suggestions for improving one's life, yet I encourage you to read the book from start to finish in order to truly grasp what Giving Room means, both in terms of how it is described within this book and how it relates to your life. Is Giving Room about being a better parent? Possibly. Is it about strengthening your relationships? Could be. Or is Giving Room about finding more happiness in your everyday life? Maybe so. But one thing is certain: Giving Room is about figuring out what you need and making shifts in your life to move toward it. It's about positive change.

I hope you enjoy reading about Giving Room and I am confident you will benefit in your own unique way.

Chapter One

GIVING ROOM IS DIFFICULT

HOLLY'S STORY: "NOT TOO MUCH JAM!"

Winter sleet and rain pound the rickety fifty-year-old apartment complex in Southside Philly. Its wooden shutters barely hang on, clinging to the mud-red brick siding like driftwood being tossed on a stormy sea. The wind howls as Holly kicks at the door of Unit 2, her home. This rarely happens. She again reaches into the pocket of her backpack and unzips the secret compartment in the bottom right corner. Searching, searching, but still no key! Tears roll down her cheeks as Holly again retraces the regimented, daily steps in her mind. . . .

The alarm clock sounds at 6:00 a.m. Quickly, though she is still half-asleep, Holly heads for the kitchen. She methodically begins pouring the coffee grounds into the coffee machine filter, then adds the water and presses the start button. Mother's coffee will be ready in no time. Next, she pops a few slices of bread into the toaster oven for herself and her sister, Katie. A sliced bagel is tossed in for her mother. Her cat, Sunny, is next. She cleans out the litter box, refills her food bowl, and gives her fresh water. On the kitchen table, Katie and Holly's homework is scattered. Like a veteran assembly-line worker at an automotive plant, Holly organizes her sister's homework. She knows her sister's daily schedule at school to a tee: first numbers, then letters, then there is story time. Holly throws her own books and assignments haphazardly into her backpack and heads for the bathroom. She rushes through her grooming ritual: wash the face, brush the teeth, comb the hair, and throw on some clothes. Holly then allows herself to go to the bathroom.

Katie is then awakened. It's 6:40 a.m. As Holly departs their bedroom, she barks the usual commands: "Clothes, socks, and shoes are at the bottom of bed. Get dressed and get in the bathroom." Back in the kitchen, she butters the toast, wraps it carefully in a washcloth, and shoves it into her pocket. Holly hears Katie fumbling around in the bedroom. All it takes to get Katie back on track is a stern look from her big sister. Mother's bagel is placed on a plate and strawberry jam and butter are applied. Not too much jam! Mother doesn't like too much jam. Mother's coffee is then prepared. Exactly two and one-half teaspoons of sugar. No milk. No cream.

Holly glances down at her wristwatch, suddenly alarmed that twenty minutes have elapsed since waking her sister.

"That's impossible! It should only be 6:56 a.m., not 7:00 a.m.!" she worries aloud. Holly knows she is on the clock now and running dangerously late. Forced to rush through the final and most delicate of steps in her morning ritual, Holly stops abruptly in the middle of the hallway. Like a boxer trying to pump up for a prizefight, Holly aggressively rubs her face with both hands, then shakes out her hands and arms. Slowly she begins to tiptoe toward her mother's bedroom. She twists the doorknob and it squeaks; Holly freezes, her whole body cringing. Mother moans but fortunately doesn't wake. The stench from the room is overwhelming, a combination of her mother not showering for a week, cigarette smoke, and the half-eaten pizza, moldering on the bedside table.

Holly taps her mother on the shoulder and whispers in her ear, "Mommy, your coffee and bagel are ready." Her mother doesn't move. Holly whispers louder, "Mommy, your coffee and bagel are ready." Her mother begins to stir. Now is the moment of truth. Holly's heart races and sweat beads her little brow. *Which Mommy will it be this time? Nice Mommy? The Mommy who reads to us, sings songs with us, and hugs us? The Mommy who tells me she loves me? The Mommy who says I'm a big girl and that she is proud of me? Or will it be Mean Mommy, who hits us, calls us names, and, worst of all, the Mommy who stays in her room and doesn't come out for days?* Lately, it's been rough. Holly and Katie have been living with "Mean Mommy" for several weeks now.

Mother's puffy eyelids slowly rise; her face is blank. Holly braces herself. After ten seconds of her mother's frozen expression, Holly's heart begins to sink. But look! Suddenly, a slight smile plays across Mother's lips. Holly promptly but carefully smiles back, gently repeating, "Mommy, your coffee and bagel are ready. Katie and I must leave now for school." Mother nods her head in a caring and reassuring manner. Feeling good vibes from Mommy, Holly takes a bold, very bold, chance. "Oh, and Mommy? Don't forget that today is Wednesday, February 2, and you have that job interview at the cleaners at 9:30 this morning. I ironed that pretty red dress for you last night. It's over there in the corner." Again, Holly braces herself. Mommy continues to nod and smile and softly says, "Thank you."

Love fills her heart as Holly goes back on the clock. She heads rapidly down the hallway and into the kitchen. Katie, all ready to go and sporting backpack and winter attire, is sitting in the kitchen chair closest to the front door. Immediately, Holly's and Katie's eyes meet. Words need not be spoken as Katie's eyes ask the familiar question: *Nice Mommy or Mean Mommy?* Holly nods her head and smiles. Katie quickly smiles back. "Let's go," Holly instructs in a confident manner. As Holly closes the front door, the biting winter wind whips across her face. She glances at her watch: 7:20 a.m. Removing the toast from her pocket, she hands Katie her piece. "Katie, go a little faster today; we're running behind." Katie nods. Holly zips her coat all the way to the top, flips up her hood, and jams her hands in her pockets. The hour-long journey to school begins. . . .

"That's it! I remember!" Holly exclaims. Katie looks at her sister with renewed hope. "Did you find the key? It's freezing out here!" Although the key's whereabouts is no longer a mystery, Holly's heart sinks. She knows she will be unable to open the door. In a trancelike monotone, she explains, "The key is on the hook in the kitchen. Mommy should be home in fifteen minutes to let us in." Katie begins to whimper. Although Holly's expression doesn't change, her little seven-year-old body is filled with nausea and anger—anger at herself. *You're smarter than that, Holly Smith!* Her brain won't let her off the hook. *You know your LAST task in the morning is to grab the key from the kitchen hook!* Holly turns around, walks over to her sister, and guides her to sit between her legs on the top step. Holly holds Katie tight and rocks her back and forth in a soothing manner.

She croons in Katie's ear, "Everything will be okay! When Mommy gets home, you'll go straight to our room and change out of your wet clothes. Put your pj's on and practice your numbers. I'll come to get you when dinner is ready." Although the day started out promising, Holly now knows it is going to end horribly. The rage her mother unleashes whenever her daughters are locked out of the apartment is predictable. But Mother's anger never stems from worry about Holly and Katie being out in the nasty weather, cold and hungry; nor does it come from frustration or guilt about not being home to greet her daughters when they return from school. Mother's fury does not even disguise sadness or regret for not coming up with alternative ways for her girls to enter the apartment. No, her anger is all about embarrassment and fear. These thoughts ran through Holly's mind as she and Katie quietly sat on the front stoop, shivering, waiting for Mother to arrive. Holly knows only too well what to expect. "God help you two damn brats if the neighbors ever saw you out here. You'd just love that, now, wouldn't you! You'd like nothing better than for that nosy bitch Mrs. Blanner to call DFS one more time! Maybe next time will be your lucky day, and they'll take you from me, and you'll never see me again, EVER!" Holly's self-castigating anger continues to build in her young brain, giving her no room. *Damn you, Holly! Damn you! You can't even remember to bring the house key!*

THE ODDS ARE AGAINST US

As a rookie psychotherapist, I learned pretty quickly one of life's harshest truths: People don't like to change! Sad but true, change is something most people steer clear of. Much research over the years backs up this "fight against change" and reveals that the average number of times an individual attends a first therapy session is less than one! It seems that after they make the phone call and schedule the first appointment, many people simply don't even show up! Now that's resistance!

I often communicate this fundamental problem to my clients very early in treatment. As I explain that the odds are against them to realize real positive growth, most patients nod their heads and smile, and I know they're thinking: *Oh, sure, but I'm different. I'm enthusiastic about changing! I'm hurting too much inside; I am ready to embrace change! And I'm paying you damn good money, so I BETTER change!* Although I always present this caveat, I make sure to end the session on an optimistic note. Some people return, willing to work on changing, and the therapeutic process works over time. Others stay stuck in their behaviors, and no matter how wonderful a therapist you are, the person's emotional struggles stay engrained.

Doing something new or in a different way is always difficult. From infancy throughout our entire lives, we resist change. The young child apprehensively rocks back and forth, back and forth, back and forth, in an almost hypnotic rhythm, so hesitant is she to crawl for the first time. The five-year-old clings to her mother's side, biting vigorously on her Winnie the Pooh shirt as they enter the kindergarten classroom for the first time. "Mommy, please just stay with me!" she pleads, as tears stream down her face. The grungy-looking, nervous high school sophomore paces outside the school two weeks before the first formal dance, so anxious is he to get up the nerve to ask cute little Susie to accompany him. At age thirty-two, the promising young college graduate, a mere ten years out of school, finds that the only real excitement in her life is complaining with colleagues about their dead-end jobs and burying that frustration and depression every Friday and Saturday evening at happy hour. And then there is the ubiquitous codependent partner who, for thirty years, has continued to suffer the vicious cycle of her narcissistic husband, who violently dumps his empty feelings of worthlessness on her through verbal degradation and physical abuse. The typical makeup period following these abusive episodes passes like clockwork, and the storm hits again and again. Doing something different would be very, very difficult. Most people do not like change.

As human beings, our natural tendency is not to take that bold step into the unknown of change. Patterns are set early in life, and as we move through the developmental stages, we sometimes feel like passengers on a runaway train, unable to brake or change the train's direction. Temporary changes may occur. We say, "It's time for my New Year's resolution! I'm going to lose fifty pounds!" Yet too often in this day and age true lasting change just doesn't stick. Of course, it's not simply "normal development" that hinders change and positive

29

growth in life. Other circumstances, trauma, for example, lock in our paralytic states of being.

Sometime within the first thirty minutes of meeting a client, I usually ask, "Now this might seem like a weird question, but has there ever been any type of traumatic experience that has occurred in your life? You know, something that you might look back on and say, 'Yeah, that was really bad, that was really unexpected, that was really awful?'" Do you know why I use the word *weird*? Webster's dictionary defines *weird* as "suggesting the operation of supernatural influences." To me, the word *weird* is esoteric and vague. When clients hear the words *weird question*, an uneasy, mysterious feeling is immediately triggered, yet because of the ineffable nature of the word, it leaves room for the clients to search their memory banks for intense feelings that may be hidden by their history.

Some clients blow off the question and say, "No, nothing really comes to mind." But others will ponder the question. At such times, the mood in the room changes as tales of dysfunctional relationships, abuse, medical issues, and many other troubling events come tumbling out. Very often, it doesn't take a clinical psychologist to put two and two together. Clearly, many of those traumatic events and situations are seriously impacting people's current level of happiness. The connection of the past to the present is often clear to clients as well. In frustration, one will gasp, "I know my father's death during my adolescence impacted how I relate to men! I just can't fix it!" Or with a smirk, a client will respond with a sense of accomplishment, "Dr. Castro, don't you find it interesting that I was attacked by a vicious dog when I was five and yet now, as an adult, I am the owner of a dog-training facility? I just love dogs!" Childhood trauma can impact one's adulthood in many ways that aren't always negative. Paralysis, fear, and loss can be one individual's avenue to a thriving business. Of course, Freudians would say that my dog trainer is experiencing a "reaction formation," but I like to think of it as an expression of the indomitable human spirit.

MY MEMORY—AND OTHER PSYCHOLOGICAL PROCESSES— ESCAPE ME

It's clear that our inability to remember everything about our past, whether riddled with trauma or not, often impedes healthy psychological growth. Doesn't it make sense that if one could remember past experiences in a more clear and rational way (without the pain, frustration, fear, anger, and other emotions that surround them), it would be helpful to use those events as springboards to future growth? Then maybe we wouldn't always make the same mistake twice, three times, four times, and on and on through life! As the old saying goes, "If someone lets you down and breaks your trust, shame on them. If that same person does it twice, shame on you!" Remembering our past in a constructive and meaningful way—not in an obsessive or self-destructive way—would inspire all of us to make better choices in life. Our relationships would be healthier and our self-esteem would flourish.

Every day in my office I ask my first-time clients for some information about their childhood: "So if I was looking down on you and your family when you were a kid during dinnertime, what would it be like? Who would be present? Who would be talking? Who would be silent?" Or I ask something more traditional during a psychological intake, such as "How would you describe your mother and father as you were growing up?" and "Tell me about their marriage."

Much has been written over the years about the struggle with *time* and *memory* when it comes to childhood development, and it isn't surprising that I struggle to remember the names of my grade school teachers. Yet, the few things I do remember remain crystal-clear in my mind to this day. Whether you remember all of your childhood or very little, there are important moments or experiences that shape who you are today and affect your capacity to change.

Take, for example, Eric, a forty-one-year-old patient who has a vivid childhood memory of his mother sitting him down at the kitchen table, pointing her index finger in his face, and screaming, "All men are shit!" When Eric's father got home from work, his mother would complain to him about how badly Eric had behaved. This led to Eric's father barging into his room with belt in hand, another childhood incident Eric remembers clearly. It is not surprising that Eric struggles to connect with other men and has no male friends.

However, Eric also has memories of his violin lessons with a sweet old man named Mr. Thomas. Eric begins to tear up when he tells me, "Mr. Thomas would pat my back and tell me I had a gift for music and that he was proud of me." Today, Eric is one of the most accomplished violinists in the Midwest.

The pioneers on the study of impact of memory are the psychoanalytic theorists who described the importance of defense mechanisms. Freud first introduced the concept of defenses (he used the word *repression* interchangeably with *defense*) in 1894 as a kind of trick the mind plays to protect us from inappropriate wishes and to keep these taboo thoughts and feelings in the unconscious. Freud's daughter, Anna, in

1936 expanded on the idea of defenses when she wrote the classic book *The Ego and the Mechanisms of Defense*. Rather than expound on the phenomenon of repression that her father brought to light, Anna Freud detailed specific defense mechanisms such as denial, projection, and—my personal favorite— "undoing." In a very simple and general way, defense mechanisms were seen, and still are seen, as a way for the mind to protect us from intense, powerful feelings and memories, as well as personal shortcomings.

In the book *Psychoanalytic Terms and Concepts*, the *undoing* defense is defined as "ritualistically removing the offensive act, sometimes by atoning for it." But let me get away from the psychobabble and give you my own definition of *undoing*. Undoing occurs when something bad or extreme or severe has occurred in one's life, and, because of the harshness of the event or situation or relationship, the individual feels the need to "undo it" or atone for it by doing something else that is close to the opposite of the negative event. A great example of this, and one I see so frequently in my practice, has to do with parenting. The parents who are sitting in my office were raised the "traditional way." They consistently describe their upbringing like this: "My dad was the breadwinner and my mom stayed at home and raised us. We were told, 'Children should be seen but not heard.' You never questioned my parents. If you questioned their authority, they would unleash severe mental and physical punishment."

As I gather history from these parents, it becomes clear that they had "no voice" as children. They were simply not Given Room as kids to question and explore the meaning of rules at appropriate times. The message was "You do not speak unless I speak to you!" They were not allowed to use their creativity to grow if it did not fit neatly into the rigid boundaries of home rule. They would hear frequent condemnations such as "You do *not* do such things under my roof!" The few times these kids did break out of the box of parental assumptions and rules, they were shoved back in forcibly. Their only choice was to "follow the program and keep your mouth shut!"

After hearing about their childhoods, I am compelled to ask the question that stops these parents in their tracks: "So how do you guys handle discipline with your eight-year-old son, Billy, and your three-year-old daughter, Susie?"

Typically, the parents will look at each other and start stumbling over their words. The mom stutters, "Well, that's where we have a problem. I mean, we do discipline them, but nothing seems to work."

Dad jumps in. "We've tried time-outs. We've even grounded them, but things seem to be getting worse."

And then they really start to open up. "Dr. Castro, they are very disrespectful. They scream at us. They throw things and yell, '*I don't have to do it! I hate you! Get out of my room!*'"

I flesh out their story: "Let me guess. Sometimes they will even hit you, or they may break stuff in your house when they are really mad?"

These parents look at me in astonishment as if I were a Peeping Tom at their windows, watching every sad scene. Parents get extremely emotional at this point. They tear up and sigh in frustration. Most parents declare with exasperation, "We need help!"

So a new process begins to unfold, the process of teaching these parents that it's appropriate to parent with the conviction that there is a hierarchy in the family. I teach that, at times, it is okay to simply "explain" to your child, "Because I'm the parent and you're the child." And it's okay to enforce this authority. You see, I've never met parents who didn't really want the absolute best for their children. Parenting is such hard work, and when you combine this hard work with the rigidness that many adults experienced in their own childhoods and, in some cases, the extreme sense of entitlement we give to kids today, it is a recipe for disaster. The "undoing" process in so many families has completely sabotaged healthy child rearing.

The irony of defense mechanisms is that while they are necessary psychic tools, they may also hinder a person from Giving Themselves Room to grow emotionally in life. Defenses are good in the sense that they protect us from the intense emotions that would bombard our minds 24/7. Seriously, without defense mechanisms, most of us would spend all day and night fighting off negative thoughts. Defense mechanisms naturally keep us from going insane! Whether it is a heavy-duty defense that wipes out memory (such as denial), or a more lighthearted defense that just blurs memory and the truth (such as rationalization), defenses are needed to provide stability in life. Yet Giving Room to let down one's own defenses is a vital step in staying emotionally healthy. It is a risky endeavor, yet required for emotional growth. Letting down defenses that have been built and strengthened over a lifetime is no easy task. One can't just say, "I'm doing away with my defenses now." Giving Room is recognizing that we have defenses and understanding how they affect our daily lives. Taking the time and Creating the Space to accept this about ourselves allows us to think about new ways to change our behavior to achieve the desired result—assuming, of course, we really do want to change.

This back-and-forth of remembering and learning from our experiences in a coherent manner, as opposed to tucking them away, out of sight and out of mind, is the proverbial dance that usually occurs in therapy. When all goes well, therapeutic trust emerges over the first few sessions. The client begins to think, *I can really talk to this guy (or gal). He seems to understand me. And it really seems like he cares. Plus, he seems like a cool dude with his long, straggly hair.* So the client, Bob, takes a risk. "I'm a little nervous saying this, but I feel that I'm starting to learn about why I behave the way I do, so I figure I should tell you about this situation that happened years ago that I haven't thought about in ages. For some reason my gut tells me it's important to look at. So, here goes. . . ." And suddenly the mood in the room shifts. It's a calm yet focused mood, filled with intense emotion. I may even see a few tears fall from this person's eyes.

As the session moves on, clarity and understanding may dawn. Unfortunately, I must always say, "I'm aware of our time. I will see you next week."

The client stands up feeling a little nervous, but smiles and nods in a manner that communicates "Thank you, we took a big step today."

Like a good coach with a hardworking athlete, psychologists get excited for patients who do the work prescribed during therapy. Sometimes we're quite surprised by the people who end up doing the work. For example, a week later, right before Bob's appointment, I'm pumped! *Wow, this client is really doing the work! Good for him for taking that risk last week! Way to go for discussing some very vulnerable feelings!*

Bob sits down on my couch and immediately starts going through his week. "Not much new this week. Work is still work. My wife is still annoying, but I love her. And not much excitement going on, except of course deer season is right around the corner. . . ." I sit there, listening, minute after minute, wondering when the shift will take us back to the good stuff from last week. As the minutes continue to roll, it becomes increasingly apparent that the chance of my client making "the shift" today is unlikely.

I am not too bothered by this "light session." It is typical in therapy for the process of discovery and movement to ebb and flow. But I want to make sure last week's session with Bob is at least acknowledged. So I jump in with "Not to change the subject (I often start with that disingenuous statement—"not to change the subject"—when I'm leading a therapy session, even though my exact intention *is* to change the subject!), and we can get back in a minute to discussing the new compound bow you plan on using to take down that twelve-point buck, but I was wondering how you were feeling about our last session."

Bob looks at me blankly. "What do you mean?"

I respond nonchalantly, "Well, you know. Like, when you were leaving last session. How did you feel?"

Again he seems confused. "Now when was our last session?"

"Well, it was last week on the same day at the same time. Just as it always is."

He's clearly searching, but evidently nothing is standing out, and now I'm the one who's really depressed! "Um, I'm thinking I felt okay. Other than that, I can't really remember a whole heck of a lot from last week."

Dejected and temporarily defeated, I ask, "Now what color did you say that compound bow is?"

CREATING SPACE FOR HAPPINESS

HOLLY'S STORY: "IN JESUS' NAME WE PRAY. AMEN."

As childhood passed and the years rolled by, Holly's maturity and responsibilities grew exponentially. By age four, she already possessed the daily living skills of a responsible adult. She had grown proficient in changing her younger sister's diaper and feeding her milk and cereal every three hours. She flew through the laundry like a seasoned laundress, always making sure to separate the whites from the colors. Her cooking skills were more than adequate. Katie would let out a piercing laugh and clap her hands in excitement whenever Holly lit the stove with a match. Lighting the stove became a ritual for the girls, and they looked forward to it every night. *POOF!* The mysterious blue flames quickly appeared. The girls would smile at each other—one of the rare moments Holly would actually allow herself a smile.

The evening routine for Holly and Katie started at 7:30. Holly bathed Katie first, thoroughly cleaning her sister from head to toe.

Katie would occasionally put up a fight. "No, I don't want my hair washed today!" But her defiant outbursts were almost always short-lived. It was "the look" that knocked Katie back into compliance. Harsh words were never needed when it came to Holly parenting her younger sister. Katie had learned from Day One that, in the end, if she followed Holly's instructions and allowed her big sister to take on the mothering role, things would turn out better.

One time, Katie actually took it too far and screamed, "Mom! Holly's not cleaning me right! Mommy, I need you! Mommy, I need you!" The situation turned into the nightmare of all nightmares for Katie and for Holly.

The look of pure evil and rage that shot from Mother's eyes as she entered the bathroom, leather belt in hand, is the look that neither Katie nor Holly will ever forget. The beating was brutal that night, leaving both girls with bright red welts up and down their backs and bottoms. But it was the eyes—the savage eyes of a crazed animal—that produced the most painful blows, leaving deep scars in the girls' little brains.

During a typical evening, after Katie's pajamas were on and she was engrossed in looking at pictures in her favorite Dr. Seuss book, Holly would step into the brown-stained bathtub. Allowing herself only sixty seconds to wash up, she was usually out of the tub and dry within another fifty seconds. By 8:00 p.m., Katie was tucked into bed and Holly would lead prayers: "Dear Jesus, please have Mommy come home safely tonight. Please let her be Nice Mommy when she gets home and have her go right to bed. Jesus, please make sure we have money and food. Please make sure we do all the things we *have to do* tomorrow. And Jesus, if Mommy is going to be Mean Mommy, please don't let it last too long. In Jesus' name we pray."

And in unison, the girls would say, "Amen." Holly would kiss her sister on the forehead and snuggle up against her until Katie was asleep. The day would end for Holly as she practiced her letters and numbers before falling asleep, completely exhausted. By age four, Holly was reading on a third-grade level.

To Holly, these childhood duties and immense responsibilities were normal, and she took them very seriously. But it was school and its environment of learning that was Holly's escape. The moment she entered Westport Elementary, the tightness and nauseous feelings deep in her stomach disappeared. Her breath slowed to a regular rhythm and the little muscles throughout her body softened. She made it a point every day as she entered school to stop and gather herself. That's when the transformation from intense physical anxiety to normalcy would begin. She enjoyed these five to ten seconds. It was the only time during the day when her body and mind would give her permission, would Give Her Room, to be off the clock. "Breathe! It is your time. You are free for now."

THE RAT RACE

What happens to the rat once the Rat Race ends? Answer: The rat dies! I love that saying—even if it is rather morbid—because that is the reality for so many of us today. But it doesn't have to be! Just like the little rodent that scurries through his maze, hyperfocused on making that sharp turn around the corner and finding his treat at the end, we humans put on our own set of blinders and anxiously sprint through life. The Italian saying *"Domani, domani, sempre domani,"* meaning "Tomorrow, tomorrow, always tomorrow," expresses the tunnel vision of our society. We are always looking out for what's in the future while life passes us by.

Don't you sometimes wish you were back in the 1950s, living the life of the family on the TV show *Leave It to Beaver?* It's not the "Oh, life is so wonderful" outlook of the characters with warm smiles on their faces that intrigues me. No, for me, the foundation of *Leave It to Beaver* is the portrayal of a simple, slow, stress-free world, and that is so damn appealing! The family wakes up and congregates at the breakfast table. While June Cleaver contentedly maneuvers about the kitchen preparing the eggs, toast, and bacon, Ward Cleaver leisurely flips through the daily newspaper. The kids finally lumber down the stairs and join their parents at the carefully set table. And what do you know? They all actually have a conversation with one another. Imagine that! A conversation over a morning meal with your family members that lasts for more than thirty seconds! The conversations aren't deep. They are not filled with passionate problem-solving advice given by Mom and Dad. These conversations are slow and light. It is a time for the family to connect in a ritualistic yet carefree manner before they head off for their daily duties. It is a place to feel grounded and loved.

In today's world, this type of breakfast is virtually extinct. In fact, many of us just skip the breakfast (and, naturally, the conversation). There is no time for breakfast. Too many places to go, people to see. Too many carpools to tend to. In my case, too many clients to treat! And this boulder (called the Rat Race) rolls downhill and picks up speed throughout the day. Every day. You rush to get the kids to school on time. Then you rush off to work and come flying in to your workplace ready to hit the ground running. And in the blink of an eye, you glance over at the clock and—how is it possible? The workday is over. Immediately, you are filled with anxiety, knowing you must be in the car in the next two minutes or you'll be "fined" for being late by the after-school care facility currently tending to your kids. Speeding home, luck is on your side as all the traffic lights turn green (although you did run a couple of yellows). The kids are retrieved, belted into the minivan, and then off you go, all while the boulder rolling downhill picks up speed! As you exit the school, you take a deep breath and peer through the rearview mirror. "So, kids, how was your day?" "Well, Mom, we've gotta stop right away to pick up a poster board for my science project. . . ."

Unfortunately, by this point you are exhausted and on the verge of checking out cognitively. But you can't! The Rat Race is still going; you're still on the clock! "We'll get to that soon, honey. I'm going to want to hear all about that project, but right now what I need you to do is put on your soccer clothes and shin pads and cleats."

"But, Mom, I'm not supposed to change in the car! I was taught in school that . . ."

You interrupt loudly. "Billy! I am driving very, very carefully, so just take the seatbelt off, get dressed, and then get back in your seat!"

The car ride to the soccer field turns silent except for Susie whimpering in the backseat, "Mommy, I'm so hungry! I don't think I had much for breakfast this morning!"

IMPRISONED BY GUILT

The thing I love most about my professional life is that every therapeutic hour is unique. I have been blessed with the insight and breadth of training that allows me to treat many different types of people struggling with an array of issues. I try to be diligent about not scheduling too many similar clients with similar issues back-to-back. I tend to enjoy my job more when I mix things up hour by hour.

One hour I may be playing house on the floor with little Joey. As Joey arranges the figures to represent the members of his family, strong emotions of sadness and jealousy surface and are processed. Joey's facial expressions take on the characters of the little "brother and sister" dolls clenched in his hands, as they argue over who is granted the privilege of setting the table for dinner. Even though my door is closed, Joey yells loudly enough for my secretary in the other room to hear. "No, Mary, it is NOT your turn! Get out of my way or I'll hit you!" It is a release for Joey. Almost magically, the intensity of his obsessive-compulsive symptoms dissipates. His teacher later notices the change.

The next hour, a teenager spends much of the first twenty minutes discussing the sound system she just bought for her black 2000 Mustang. She is so proud of this car and continues to work twenty-plus hours a week at a local car wash to have the resources to sculpt the car into her ultimate image, while staying on top of her academics and maintaining a 3.5 grade-point average. This is how we usually begin our sessions, and it is a time for this attractive high school tomboy to talk excitedly about the one thing she can control. Our "car talk" ritual goes a long way toward helping her to feel comfortable with me. As the doctor-patient relationship strengthens over time, the length of time spent on breeze-shooting shortens, and the transition into discussing her parents' dysfunctional marriage and her lack of control over it begins.

The following hour is William, a forty-one-year-old man who was referred to me by an attending psychiatrist at the local hospital. His paranoia and paralyzing anxiety about getting into his car and driving is so thick that it fills the therapy room. Tears glaze his eyes as he describes the frustration and self-loathing he feels for letting down his wife and "being a failure." He shakes his head in fury. "I just don't get it! For twenty-five years I drove all over the place making deliveries. But now I'm scared to death to get on that highway. I just know something bad is going to happen!" It takes a while to calm William down and get him focused on the relaxation techniques and the desensitization behavioral approach (gradual exposure to the feared situation) we have worked on week after week. By the end of the session, he is ready to continue making baby steps. He is able to reflect on the gradual changes that have occurred over the months. First it was just sitting in the car, then starting the car, then driving to the end of the driveway. I assure him that getting on that highway is not too far off.

My final hour of the workday might best be described as "Marriage on the Rocks." The stern look of John, the silent husband with his arms crossed, communicates quite clearly that he is guarded and has no interest in therapy. He becomes more and more furious as his wife, Kelly, rattles off the numerous instances of John's lack of sensitivity and love for her. She complains, "Damn you! Why do you always have to go golfing Saturday morning?! Have you ever once thought of taking me out for brunch and having a normal conversation with me?"

As usual, John doesn't respond and rolls his eyes with a sigh. But by the end of the session, he can no longer hold back. He impulsively bites back. "Have a normal conversation with you!? All you do is bitch and moan about how I can't do anything right! Why the hell would I want to have ANY conversation with you, let alone a normal one?"

And then there is silence, and they both look at me as if to say, "So what the hell do we do now?"

I hesitate before beginning the work of teaching these partners that in a successful relationship, the partners communicate in a slightly healthier manner.

But if I were to be asked, "So, as a therapist dealing with all the different issues people bump up against in life, what would you say is the hardest thing to change? What is your clients' greatest challenge?" I would have to say this: It is not assisting John and Kelly to Give Room by expressing their needs in a nonaccusatory and straightforward way. It is not tending to and Creating Space for young Joey's sibling rivalry that makes him feel like his life has been turned upside down after the birth of his baby sister. Nor is it dealing with a teenager's issues of control or a former deliveryman's struggles with anxiety—these dynamics are far from being untreatable. No, the most difficult and frustrating challenge a therapist can face boils down to one word. This dread word makes me shiver to even put it on the page! The word is *guilt*. Guilt is one of the primary emotional blockages in life that stands in the way of Giving Room to change. When an individual has been mired in guilt throughout his life, that guilt is like glue. Becoming unstuck from guilt is almost impossible. Remember the old Krazy Glue ad about the construction guy who glued his hardhat to a steel beam and just hung suspended from his hat for hours? Now that's being stuck! And let me tell you something, guilt is a lot stronger even than Krazy Glue!

The Monster Guilt Blob forces people to do the most unbelievable things, things that intellectually don't make sense. Over and over, I observe really smart people ruining everything they have hoped and worked for just because they feel inadequate or undeserving. A nagging voice screams, "You are doing something wrong! You don't deserve this! Don't do it, Bad Boy! Don't do it, Bad Girl!" Guilt can sabotage people getting what they want in life. It can chew its way through our lives as subtle and sometimes not so subtle self-destructive actions. Imagine that you are in line for an impressive promotion when suddenly, for "no reason," you somehow manage to get yourself fired. Or, you have found the love of your life, but the next thing you know, she is writing you a Dear John letter. Or, for the past several months, you've worked through the rigorous training to realize your lifelong dream of running the Chicago Marathon. Who would have guessed that three weeks before the big race you would go on a drinking binge with your old college buddies? You finish the race, but it's just not the experience and performance you were hoping for. Your mind and body were not where they needed to be.

Guilt is also responsible for the intense, often vicious cycle of "taking the hit" for others—a recurring theme ruining many people's lives. We hear so many people justify this behavior by rationalizing: "I was born to help others. It's simply who I am!" Yet when the people in our lives keep on taking and taking, without looking out for *our* needs, we are filled with resentment. Angrily, we vent, "Screw the owners of this damn company. I worked sixty-plus hours last week even though it is written that a forty-hour workweek is the max. I am constantly giving them a Mercedes for the price of a Hyundai! We are going on three days, THREE DAYS, and not one of those thoughtless jerks has said to me, 'Great job.' And to top it off, my wife is pissed because I wasn't home for dinner all week!"

But when you ask this guy two weeks later, "How many hours have you been working lately?"

He casually responds, "Oh, about sixty hours a week."

"And why so many hours?" you ask.

He looks at you as if you are dumb as a rock. "Because I don't want anyone to be annoyed with me."

One of the main reasons guilt is such a struggle for so many people is that there are few descriptive words people can wrap their minds around when asked to describe their "guilty feelings." The struggle with understanding and articulating guilt makes it difficult for us to work through guilty feelings and move forward. It is usually easier for a person to feel and express an emotion like anger: "You really pissed me off today! Get the hell out of my face! Why is that geezer in the car in front of me moving like a tortoise?" and on and on. Anger is often accompanied by a physical action—like punching the steering wheel—which underscores the act of expression. Furthermore, it is easier to express anger because it is so often "other directed." With guilt, on the other hand, it is difficult to "pass the buck" on to someone else. Verbal expression is difficult when you feel guilty about an action or perceived failure for which you are responsible. There is no "other" to get mad at—only yourself!

The same is true with feelings of sadness or grief. We can put words to these emotional responses so much easier than we can for guilty feelings: "I weigh one hundred and fifty pounds, but my depression is so heavy I feel like I weigh three hundred pounds! And if I keep eating these damn bon-bons all day I am going to weigh three hundred pounds! Help!" Or a client might say, "The loss of my mother hits me once in a while throughout the day like a forty-foot wave. It leaves me feeling lost and hopeless, and all I can do is hide under my blanket and cry. Please stop the waves!"

But when guilt is the primary underlying emotion causing problems, those people who suffer are often silent. This silence is due to the lack of knowledge of what is causing all the turmoil or the feeling of paralysis in their life. When confronted with their feelings of guilt and shame, these patients can deftly sidestep the real issue. For example, Steve feels that he has let down his brother because he wasn't there to support him during his divorce, a time of great need. When asked how he feels about it, Steve tells me, "My brother is a good guy, but his wife can be a real bear sometimes. . . ."

I reply, "What I am asking you, Steve, is: What does it feel like in your belly, really deep down in your gut, when you start to imagine that you could have done more for your brother during his times of need?"

It might be surprising to hear, but even a direct approach often results in a confused look, as Steve responds with something evasive like "I don't know. But speaking of their divorce, did I ever tell you about the time when his wife started spying on him in the bathroom?" I will often ask clients, like Steve, to slow down and not respond so quickly to my question. I say, "Steve, before you answer, I want you to repeat the question to me." Once Steve understands the question, I direct him as follows: "Now, Steve, close your eyes, take a deep breath, and Give Yourself Room to ponder the question. Create the Space to really think about it before you respond." As a therapist, cracking this nut can take a long time, but by slowing down the therapeutic process at crucial points, clients can begin to Give Room to confront the source of their guilt. In Steve's case, he can start down the path to forgiving himself while admitting responsibility and becoming a better person for it.

The intense emotional anguish caused by guilty feelings is also in part due to the likelihood that, on some level, the individual actually should be feeling a little bit guilty. A forensic psychologist and good friend of mine, Dr. Rick Scott, recently pointed out that there is usually some basis in truth when a person feels guilty. The issue isn't always whether the person *should* or *shouldn't* feel guilty. The problem has to do with the intensity of the guilt the person is taking in. In other words, the individual usually takes on far too much responsibility—and therefore feels a disproportionate amount of guilt—for the situation at hand.

For example, Susan, a hardworking mom putting in fifty hours a week at work while desperately trying to parent her four kids, came into my office dejected and angry. She'd recently discovered that her seventeen-year-old (selfish, spoiled-rotten brat) daughter was bragging to her friends that whenever she needs money to go shopping for new clothes, she just takes a few crisp twenties out of her mother's money jar. Susan gasped, "Can you believe it!? I give that kid whatever she wants, and she just spits in my face and has the audacity to crow about it to her friends!"

As we begin to discuss how to address the issue with her daughter, Susan cuts me off and excitingly starts recounting the guilt-riddled tirade she dumped on her daughter, "Oh, no, Dr. Castro. Don't you worry! I really gave it to her!"

This response really got me fired up! I inquired, "Well, what did you do? What did you say?"

Susan replied, "Let me tell you, I gave it to her for almost two hours straight, while tears ran down my face, about how hard I work and that I haven't had enough money for a new pair of jeans in twelve years!" Susan went on and on, explaining to me how she smeared layer upon layer of guilt all over her daughter: "I told her how my bones ache and crack because I'm on my feet twelve hours a day at work. I even made her look at my ankles to show her how swollen they are!" Susan proudly lets me know that by the end of their "discussion," her daughter was sobbing.

Clearly, Susan's daughter needs to know that what she did was wrong, and I do think it is okay to point out to this self-

49

centered teenager that her mom worked hard for that money. As my friend Dr. Scott has noted, there is usually some valid reason for feeling guilty. Certainly, Susan's daughter did something wrong and should feel bad about it. But this should not be the main focus of Susan's conversation. Susan's daughter, on some level, already knows it is wrong to take money and that her mother works hard and sacrifices for her. This seventeen-year-old kid is not a sociopath completely lacking in remorse and empathy for others. She does not take any pleasure in inflicting pain on people and she certainly knows the difference between right and wrong. Rather than making her daughter feel guilty, Susan needs to hold her daughter accountable for her actions. Susan's child has never really felt the consequences of her actions.

I question Susan. "So did you punish her for stealing your money?" Susan gets a somewhat confused look on her face. "Um . . . yeah, I think so. Oh, yeah, I told her she was grounded for two weeks."

I call Susan on the carpet. "So you mean to tell me, Susan, that you did not let your daughter go out last weekend with her friends?"

Sheepishly, Susan admits that her daughter went to the movies both nights. I ask, "And how did she get the money for the movies, Susan?" Without missing a beat she reveals, "Well, I just gave her twenty bucks from the money jar."

Now who is feeling guilt, the mom or the daughter?

Giving Room is a twofold process when it comes to Susan and her daughter. First, by teaching Susan about consistent parenting techniques that focus on holding her daughter accountable for her actions, Susan's daughter learns to Give Room and Create the Space for instilling a positive sense of responsibility in life. Second, through our discussion about guilt and how it impacts all of us, Susan is helped to Give Herself Room to recognize the guilt she may be feeling for not holding her daughter responsible for her own actions and failing to discipline her accordingly.

The purpose of this story is not simply to discuss discipline and follow-through as a parent. It's more to show the unevenness between guilt and accountability. If Susan were to continue this pattern of pounding the guilt into her daughter over and over and over again when her daughter commits a selfish and thoughtless act, her daughter might slowly start to change her behavior. But this "positive change" of thinking more about the needs of others would be fueled by intense worry and fear of doing something wrong as opposed to "It's just the right thing to do," or "I want my mother to feel happy." In the end, intense, over-the-top guilt works, but the price is steep.

So, I bet you're feeling just a little unsettled after reading some of the myriad reasons why people don't change. And I'm sure some of you are thinking, "Oh, that's great. I'm not just struggling with one of those things. I've got them all!" I can imagine the pessimistic outlook some of you might have. Yet it's important for you to understand that, as we cruise along this path called life, the longer we walk and the more experiences we have, the harder it is to change directions. Research proves you can teach an old dog new tricks, but it is a heck of a lot harder!

I want your eyes to be wide open to the truth that the traumas we all experience in life—whether they are large or small—do indeed hinder healthy development. It's important for all of us to be well aware that our memories, or lack of them, can be a roadblock to movement and growth. We all need to be confronted with the reality that if our life is a Rat Race, true happiness is passing us by, and we may eventually end up dying with bitterness and regret. Finally, I need you to understand that guilt is the mother of all stumbling blocks; it grips us and prevents many from experiencing a truly fulfilling life. It is these difficult realities and existential truths that we must "turn toward" rather than away from. In doing so, we are taking the first and most important step toward change, and the vital act of Giving Room begins.

Chapter Two

GIVING YOURSELF ROOM

HOLLY'S STORY: "SPIRAL BREAK"

Holly couldn't take it anymore. As she walked swiftly down the school's main corridor to the nurse's office, she held her right arm close to her body, in pain. Tears streamed down her cheeks as she muttered, "Darn it! Darn it!" Her skin was deathly cold and she shook uncontrollably. In between her tears, Holly's rage erupted, and she slammed the side of her fist into a locker and released a tribal scream. The pain was so fierce that she abruptly stopped and gasped for breath. Pushing herself, she caught her breath and continued down the corridor.

This morning, before school, Holly had doctored herself. She wrapped an old sheet around her neck and elbow and circled it underneath her sweater and around her skinny waist four times, fashioning a homemade sling to secure the injured arm. All morning, the other kids had been giggling at her for wearing a sweater in the humid eighty-five-degree Philadelphia summer, but the sling went undetected; her plan had worked until now. The pain was just too severe to ignore.

Playing doctor was nothing new for Holly. Katie was always a willing patient. Holly would exclaim, "Okay, Katie, it's time to play doctor! Your appendix has busted and today I must operate!" Katie would giggle with excitement as her big sister systematically laid out her surgical instruments (typically, twigs and plastic scraps the girls found on their walk home from school). Once the operation had begun, Holly's demeanor was one of intense concentration. As she made the incision by scraping the sharpest twig over Katie's lower-right abdominal region, firmly enough to only raise a light-red line, Holly would loudly announce the procedures: "Preparation of the patient is complete! Commence insertion of blade precisely two and one-half inches under lower ribcage! Incision complete! Now begin removal of ruptured organ by maneuvering surgical probe along outer region of abdomen!"

Katie found it odd that her big sister would open the windows in the dead of winter during these operations, but Katie didn't freeze. Her physician, eight-year-old Dr. Smith, would wrap her patient in many blankets, leaving only the surgical area exposed. Dr. Holly Smith, however, shivered as her magical hands healed the young child's body. Katie would plead, "Holly!" and her sister would quickly shoot her a withering look. Katie corrected herself. "Oh, I'm sorry! Excuse me, *Dr. Smith*, but aren't you cold? Why don't you just shut the windows?"

Holly would answer with dignity (as her body shook). "All

operating rooms are very cold, as this allows for little chance of infection. Now let's continue."

When adults—teachers, neighbors, the mailman—would ask, "So, Holly, do you know what you want to be when you grow up? A teacher? An artist? A nurse?" Holly would answer with confidence, "I know exactly what I'm going to be when I'm grown. I am going to major in pre-med at Penn State University and then attend the University of Pennsylvania School of Medicine. It's one of the top five med schools in the country."

Jaws would drop as her listeners chuckled. "Oh, really?"

She would conclude, "I am going to become the youngest female emergency-room doctor in Pennsylvania." Holly knew all the steps it would take to become a doctor and was already becoming quite proficient in basic emergency medical skills. Securing her injured arm had been a cinch.

In school, Holly excelled in science and would frequently bug the school librarian, sixty-year-old Mrs. McDonald, and the head of the science department, young Mr. Anderson, to order more books about the human body. She would check in every morning with Mrs. McDonald before school started, asking, "Did any of the books come in?" Mrs. McDonald and Mr. Anderson were intrigued by Holly's love of medicine. They knew just enough about Holly's family struggles to realize that unless they stepped in and helped this gifted student, Holly would have little access to an education in science and medicine. Therefore, the three of them teamed up and found creative ways to fund more books. The annual book sale in the fall and the bake sale in the spring brought Holly and her two mentors together to grow the library and expand Holly's mind.

The long walk to school that morning was especially slow. Holly limped, favoring her right side, a strategy to stabilize her arm. Katie kept repeating, "Holly, I can carry your backpack! Just let me have it!"

Holly refused her sister's offer, and every few minutes the backpack would slip down her shoulder and drop to the ground. Much like a ninety-year-old woman struggling to get out of bed, she would slowly and carefully bend down, retrieve the backpack, and hoist it back over her shoulder.

Holly smiled as she entered Nurse Parker's office. Ms. Parker smiled back, figuring Holly had decided, as she had so many times before, to skip recess and "talk medicine" with her. But the facial blotches and shivering were immediate giveaways. Ms. Parker's face tightened in anger. "Holly, what's wrong?"

"Oh, I seem to have injured my arm when I slipped in the kitchen last night. I'm pretty sure there's a fracture. I think you better take a look."

Ms. Parker unwound the homemade sling, catching her breath when the severely swollen black-and-blue limb came into view. "Now you say you slipped in your kitchen? How did that happen?"

Holly wouldn't make eye contact with Ms. Parker as she answered, "Just a little water was on the floor and I slipped."

Ms. Parker had seen enough bruises, black eyes, cuts, and burns on Holly's body to know that this current injury was not accidental. And Holly was smart enough to know that Ms. Parker was aware of the abuse, but she also knew that her mentor's hands would be tied unless she told the truth. Ms. Parker said, "Listen, Holly. I'm going to ask you the same question I've asked you on all the other occasions when you've been hurt, and I need you to tell me the truth. Everything will get better if you tell me the truth. Tell me exactly what happened to your arm!"

Holly began to tremble as she shook her head, still not making eye contact. "I just slipped."

Ms. Parker was livid. Not toward Holly. Her anger burned because she knew that Holly probably had little choice but to lie. Just last year Holly had alluded to her mother "pushing Katie," causing a bruise on her sister's leg. After futile investigations by the school and the Pennsylvania Department of Family Services, all charges of abuse were dropped. Mother was not happy. The following month, Holly and Katie suffered the most frequent and vicious scoldings of their young lives. The physical pain was piercing, yet the guilt Holly endured for causing her sister to experience unnecessary pain went even deeper. Holly had sworn to herself never to mention "Mean Mommy" to anyone ever again.

Ms. Parker and Holly sat in silence in the emergency examination room, waiting for the doctor to return with the x-ray results. Both knew the pictures would show a break in the arm. Holly attempted to lighten the mood. "So, Ms. Parker, what's new with your kids? How's Bruce liking college?"

Ms. Parker sighed, not answering her question. "Holly, I am just so upset that this has happened!"

Holly quickly interrupted, "C'mon, I'll be fine! Now tell me about Bruce. You know I also want to go to Penn State when I—"

"Holly, I am not interested in talking about Bruce. I think what we really need to talk about—"

Just then, Holly's mother crashed through the door, ran to her daughter's side, and knelt down.

With tear-filled eyes, Holly's mother gently embraced her daughter with a soft hug. "My darling, how are you feeling?" she crooned, stroking Holly's hair.

Holly immediately jumped in. "Mother, I think I broke my arm when I slipped on that water in the kitchen last night."

Mother didn't blink an eye. "Oh, yes, my darling, that awful slip! You must be more careful with your water glass."

Ms. Parker could no longer hold back. Through clenched jaws she whispered, "It's amazing how a little spilled water every month or so can cause so many different types of injuries. Don't you find that interesting, Ms. Smith?"

Holly's mother continued to soothe her daughter, never taking her eyes off her. "Yes, it is unfortunate, Leslie (Mother always called her enemies by their first name). Thanks so much for bringing Holly to the hospital! You may leave now."

Ms. Parker stood up and headed for the door. As she was about to swing the door open, Dr. Myers entered the room, x-rays in hand. Ms. Parker sat back down.

Following Dr. Myers were two nurses. Seeing the nurses, Holly's heart began to race. Her eyes scanned these helpers. The first nurse had an "RN" after her name on her scrubs. *No problem with that one*, Holly thought. As she inspected the second nurse's nametag, her heart lurched. "Nancy Davila, MSW," followed by "Behavioral Health Department." Holly's eyes became watery. She knew the only reason a social worker would be present was suspicion of abuse.

Dr. Myers placed the x-rays on the table, sat down on a small rolling stool, and rolled over to Holly. She smiled with care. "Holly, you are one smart little girl. Just as you told me, the x-ray came back positive for a break in the lower radius of the arm." Holly smiled nervously. "But the results are a little confusing," Dr. Myers continued in her soothing voice. "Can you please tell me again how the break occurred?"

Holly's face was now expressionless. Like a speeding underground train with lights flashing chaotically, Holly's mind raced as she mentally scanned her medical books. She flipped through the chapters on "Radius Breaks," "Arm Injuries," "Setting of the Arm," and so on. Nothing was coming to her. Her only option was to stick to the story. "Well, as I said before, I was in the kitchen and I'd just poured a glass of water. I placed the cup on the counter but then turned around when I heard a sound and my elbow must've swung out and knocked it over. Then as I was bending down to clean up the . . ." Suddenly Holly stopped. The expressionless look reappeared. Her heart slowed to normal and she was no longer perspiring. The answer had come to her.

Mother began to shift nervously. "I thought Holly already told you how she slipped! Why are you—"

Dr. Myers cut her off with a wave of her hand. The doctor gently probed, "What then, Holly? What happened next?"

Holly gave a small smile and dropped her head as a few tears fell, landing on her thin thighs. All eyes in the room were on her. There was no more fear, just sadness. She said, "Well, I really didn't want to say but—"

In desperation, Mother cried, "Holly, you don't have to—!"

Holly interrupted her mother with an unblinking stare and said, "It's okay, Mother." She continued. "As I was saying, I was bending down to clean the spill I made when I began to slip. The part I really didn't want to say was that as I was slipping, my sister Katie was right next to me and she tried to catch me and soften the fall. Unfortunately, she grabbed my arm and it twisted as I slipped and slammed to the ground. Katie was only trying to help. It wasn't her fault." Holly raised her head, a touch of a smile on her face, yet her look was filled with sadness. "Dr. Myers, it's a spiral break, isn't it?"

Dr. Myers stared at Holly in awe, overcome by sadness. *How in the heck could a young kid know about spiral fractures? They're only discussed in a very few medical journals in articles like "Injuries Caused by Physical Abuse." How could such a small child know that the only way to experience a spiral fracture is at the hands of another? And why!? Why is she protecting her mother?* Dr. Myers leaned in toward Holly and whispered in her ear, making sure Holly's mother couldn't hear the words. "I'm so sorry."

Dr. Myers slowly stood and patted Holly on the head. "That's right, Holly. It's a spiral fracture. You're also right about becoming a doctor someday. You're going to be a wonderful doctor." Dr. Myers headed for the door, then turned around to face Holly. "I'll be back to set your arm. As I'm sure you know, setting a spiral fracture is quite a bit more painful than a typical normal break. I suggest something extra to ease the pain."

Neither the doctor nor Holly turned to Holly's mother for her thoughts. Neither were interested in her opinion. Holly responded, "If you can break a twenty-milligram tablet of Tylenol with codeine in half, that would be fine."

As Dr. Myers departed, Mother leaned over her daughter, kissed her on top of her head, and again began stroking her hair.

I CAN'T TAKE IT ANYMORE!

At some point, most of us have been dumped by someone we thought was the "love of our life." And yeah, it hurts like hell to be delivered the phrase "I just want to be friends," particularly when you're a kid. The look of mourning on the face of that fifteen-year-old who enters my office after his first girl-friend has dropped the bomb on him after six months of blissful love is enough to make my own heart break. He tries so valiantly not to shed a tear, but in the end it is inevitable. Even his body language communicates the devastation. His hands begin to shake. His voice trembles. He sobs, "I just don't understand it! She said she loved me! She said I was the one!"

We all have our ups and downs as we meander through life, yet most of us have at least one or two strong relationships that keep us going. You know, the type of relationship where you feel that the other person is "in your corner." Most of us can also recall having been involved with people in our lives who betrayed us or let us down. Truly, our needs were of little interest to these people. But overall, when it comes to relationships, it doesn't have to be one specific type of relationship that creates meaning. Whether it is a family member, an old childhood friend, a partner, our colleague, the guy behind the register at the grocery store, or the neighbor next door, it doesn't matter. Any type of relationship can bring tears to our eyes: tears of anger and sadness or tears of joy and intimacy. All relationships are important and meaningful, and the sooner we learn to embrace the significance of each type of relationship, the sooner we will realize the link between our personal growth and connecting with others.

Many of us have not had the best of experiences with employers. After being fired or laid off five times within the past eight years, you start to wonder, is there a connection between all these layoffs? Yeah, you can easily come up with the character flaws of every single boss you've ever had—you brought sunshine and they brought rain. But maybe all these negative experiences have something to do with you.

You try to forget about the conflicts at work when suddenly you are faced with more at home. For example, your kids drive you crazy, and the "imperfections" they display eat at you constantly. Just the other day I was coaching (more like hammering!) my six-year-old daughter to answer my neighbor with a confident voice when he asks her a question and to always make sure to look him in the eye when she speaks. Over and over, I explain and role-play this important social skill to her, but she continues to struggle. At times, I feel like pulling my hair out when these important life lessons don't stick with my kids. Wherever you turn, the frustrations and disappointments find you, and the little things in life just don't feel "good enough."

As the pain builds and builds, the choice to seek real change, no matter how hard change is, becomes easier to make. The fact is, life takes many of us to the point of being "sick and tired of being sick and tired." We exclaim, "Enough! I can't take it anymore!" And that is when we enter into some form of healing in the hope of bettering our lives.

That bold step of doing something different, the decision to endure change, the courage to venture forward and Give Yourself Room to take a leap into the unknown is the secret to a happier and more fulfilling life. People in the helping professions, myself included, use many techniques to assist others in Giving Room. A yoga instructor or a Tai Chi master combine the mind and body in the healing process to create a feeling of "centergy," the idea of focusing on the core. The look of calm and peace I see on my mother-in-law's face when she's just finished a yoga class is Zen-like. There is a clear difference in her demeanor and level of frustration. She definitely hears others just a little bit more attentively, and her increase in patience is obvious. The lessons in yoga class Gave Her Room to slow down her breathing, clear her mind, and be in the moment. This allowed her to focus more on other people.

An AA leader will stress the disease model and taking "one day at a time" to members who continue to move forward in recovery. The Twelve-Step Program and an active, encouraging group support give members a path and a community to support them. A program like this Gives Members Room to understand themselves and what caused their addiction as well as Giving Room to be human—to fail—and regroup when they lapse. Each person is given that feeling of "Yes, you fell off the wagon, but we still care about you and want you to succeed." Such implicit encouragement makes members want to succeed for themselves and for the group—their family.

An army drill sergeant demands 100 percent compliance as he works to physically and emotionally break down his soldiers and then gradually rebuild their self-confidence. These once-lost, insecure troops, now confident soldiers, stand shoulder to shoulder with a feeling of purpose, as graduation from boot camp nears. Here, again, a feeling of brotherhood has been built up among those similarly positioned who root for one another and lift one another up. Each Gives the Other Room to see himself or herself as part of a greater whole—the team, platoon, regiment. The soldiers are encouraged to think that when one is faltering, all suffer, and so each member has to see his or her identity as being one with the group—all succeed or fail together. Such a sense of group, of family, of brotherhood, is assuring.

Even a financial adviser, in many ways, is a healer of emotions. She remarks to her dejected client, "I know that all you think about is how much debt you're in, but we're going to fix that. Follow my lead and before you know it, you'll be landing on stable ground." Tools to change for the better are all around us. We just have to Give Ourselves Room to pick up the tools and start hammering away! Join me—let's get to it!

DE-VELCROING YOUR MIND

The years I spent in graduate school studying to become a clinical psychologist were a thrilling time for me. Class after class, I was so excited to learn about why people act and feel the way they do. The idea of learning about an individual's psychological dynamics and how life and relationships impact who they are and who they become was quite stimulating. Again and again, we would review case studies and then spend hours conversing about the patients' struggles and triumphs; how the struggles emerged in their lives and what needed to be done to reduce their pain.

There are many different theories in psychology about what causes emotional distress and dysfunctional behavior. A therapist working within a framework of existential psychology tends to focus on the philosophical question of "choices" and how the client struggles with choices throughout all phases of his or her life. A behavioral therapist looks mainly at maladaptive behavior and then draws from behavior-oriented theories, such as the modeling theory or positive/negative reinforcement. The behaviorist will use and recommend a bagful of techniques to change behavior for the better. A cognitive therapist hones in on irrational thoughts and the negative impact they have on how we feel and how we behave. Spending time learning about a client's background and history isn't at the top of the to-do list for some of the more modern cognitive behavioral therapists. They are more interested in solving the problem, not exploring the past. One time I even had a colleague, a strict cognitive therapist, tell me, "I have been working with this guy and, wow—does he ever have a ton of distorted thoughts! You name it, he has it all: black-and-white thinking and he catastrophizes everything." He went on to say, "For years now we've worked really hard to combat his irrational thoughts. And just the other day this guy comes into my office and I ask him how his weekend was and he responds, 'Oh, it was a little stressful. My twin brother was in town visiting.' I interrupted immediately, 'Twin brother? I never even knew you had a sibling.'"

Now, the leaders of the doctoral program I attended years ago would have fainted if a fellow psychologist told them he had been seeing a patient for several years and never knew the patient had a brother, let alone a twin brother! The program was run by a bunch of psychoanalysts. We're talking "old school" shrinks, and by that, I mean "Freudian old school"! And although one of Freud's most famous quotes is "Sometimes a cigar is just a cigar," I believe Freud was just trying to be funny and that deep down he truly felt that "A cigar is NEVER just a cigar! Everything has meaning!" A strict psychoanalytic/psychodynamic approach to psychological development and change centers on that statement "Everything has meaning." The exploration embarked upon by a psychodynamic therapist and his client is about finding answers. It is about finding the origin and meaning underlying the client's impulses, dreams, phobias, addictions, passions, and relationships.

I used to challenge my psychoanalytic mentors: "How can there be NO classes or clinical works that look at a more cognitive behavioral approach to therapy? The research shows it is quite effective, and, having worked in that mode during my master's program, I've seen firsthand how helpful it can be." I asked, "Haven't you had patients who want results and change NOW and aren't willing to go through a more process-oriented type of therapy that could take years?" They shrugged their shoulders. "It's just not our focus."

As the years went on, and other students became more exposed to alternative thoughts and theories of change by spending time in clinical training facilities outside the program, there were rumblings for the need to diversify thinking. Don't get me wrong: pretty much all the students, including myself, bought into the belief that a training program focusing on psychodynamics and the therapeutic process was the way to go. We understood that, for the most part, no "quick fix" can lead to *lasting* change.

But a process-oriented type of therapy was confusing to me. I already knew how to combat a client's irrational thoughts and I was skilled in coming up with creative behavioral techniques for my clients. In addition, according to my supervisors, I was pretty good at immediately joining with clients, making them feel at ease. Another big hurdle I jumped was that I had gotten past the fear and insecurities that all beginning therapists feel. I was able to ignore or dismiss any thoughts of "Who am I to help this person?! Oh, my God, I'm the one with the issues, not her!" And my personal favorite, "Oh, no! This guy is way smarter than I am. He's probably thinking I'm a moron!"

I felt that, with my past training and clinical experience, I was a few steps ahead of some of my colleagues. Still, this whole new world of "everything has meaning" made me doubt my ability to help others. As I learned, I was able to identify the pieces of the puzzle and how they fit together, but the big picture on the cover of the box eluded me. I knew I needed to have a more one-on-one discussion with a professor about "how therapy really works." So after one of my classes in Theories of Personality and Change, I approached my professor, Dr. Helena Schwartz.

Dr. Schwartz was a petite, five-foot, one-hundred-pound woman in her early seventies. She talked softly, yet confidently. She kind of reminded me of the wise Yoda character from *Star Wars*. Like many analysts, her hair was somewhat unkempt, her clothes were a little behind the times, and in between classes she seemed somewhat frazzled as she tried to figure out her next task for the day. But when class began and she started teaching, that unmistakable aura of knowing and loving her subject matter surrounded her. We students would be giddy with excitement, like kids on Christmas morning, as we waited for her lectures to start. Her presence gave off an energy that said, "You don't want to miss a word I'm saying!"

I entered her office and immediately started pouring my guts out. "Dr. Schwartz, I'm confused. You're probably not going to understand what I'm about to say because I'm doing all right in your class, but I just don't get how therapy really works." I went on to explain my bewilderment about the "transformation" one begins to experience through therapy. To me, this transformation seemed so mystical, so magical, so intangible. I couldn't wrap my arms or my mind around it. It had nothing to do with a concrete tool. It had nothing to do with advice. I couldn't fathom the idea of a therapist not giving advice. How could it be that so few words were spoken by the therapist, yet the client could leave the therapeutic hour feeling energized and more self-confident? If I was going to be a therapist, didn't I have to talk a lot more? Was it really a matter of "the truth will set you free"?

As I spoke, Dr. Schwartz listened attentively. And the more I admitted my cluelessness, the more she just smiled. When I finally ended my rant, Dr. Schwartz was silent. Continuing to smile and slowly scooting her rolling chair closer to me, she peered over her bifocals and responded, "Anthony, you know what Velcro is, don't you?"

"Uh, yeah. It's the stuff that holds my radar detector in place so I don't get any more speeding tickets, right?"

She nodded, continuing to smile. "Well, here's the deal, Anthony. All of us have had experiences in our lives that haven't been so great. Horrible events in our lives: dysfunctional relationships, disappointments, unexpected deaths, trauma, embarrassments, humiliation, you name it. I've had them and you've had them. But also, we've all had experiences that raised us up, elevated us. Things that inspired us, making us feel alive. You know, those incredible experiences that bring tears to our eyes." She stopped and moved even closer to me. "The problem, Anthony, is that all that we carry with us, both the good and bad, is all stuck together. It's all Velcroed together. Our mind is like one big ball of Velcro, and because all those great and horrible experiences are stuck together, it's hard to understand what it all means. It's hard to see how they're connected. You want to know how therapy works? Well, that's it. Therapy is about de-Velcroing the mind."

Dr. Schwartz put her hands together as if she were holding a softball, then pulled her hands apart. "A person grows when he or she can start to de-Velcro all that stuff and look at it more clearly—*really understand it; see it for what it really is.*" Dr.

Schwartz started to shake her head. "Anthony, there is nothing magical about therapy. We don't have magic wands in our back pocket that we can wave and *POOF!* Understanding and happiness begin! It's about de-Velcroing the mind, which allows us to understand, accept, and grow even just a little bit. It is our job to assist others in this all-important task."

I often think back to my time with Dr. Schwartz and our discussion about de-Velcroing the mind. As the years have flown by, I've discovered several lessons one can take from this framework of human growth. First, Dr. Schwartz made it a point to include not just bad things in life but also those wonderful inspirational moments. This is so important, folks! In order for positive, personal change to occur, it is vitally important to Give Room and recognize these joyful moments when true, incredible things happen to us. This is the essence of bowing out of the vicious Rat Race!

It's such a great and simple lesson—"Don't forget about the good in life"—even though it goes directly against what so many people in the helping professions focus on. How often do you see a psychologist in the movies or on television successfully guiding a client to embrace all the brilliant attributes and gifts in the person's life? I'll tell you how many—none! Have you ever seen Tony Soprano energized and happy, walking out of his therapist's office and truly feeling that he is "good enough" in life? Absolutely not! Okay, maybe Tony Soprano is a bad example. And, yes, I know we are talking TV and Hollywood, but this is often the case in real life as well. We as therapists, and all people in the helping professions, need to rethink our order of business and how to balance our priorities.

Sometimes during a therapy session, I'm guilty of guiding my clients to focus on the bad stuff in life. I'm telling you, I want to kick myself after such a session, thinking, *Damn! You were acting like a pit bull trial attorney, hammering that poor little defendant with question after question.*

I'd hear myself saying, "So let me get this straight, Jeffrey. Your parents never once told you they loved you as a child? Please expand." Or, "Kerry, your dad actually used to punch you in the back of your head for no reason whatsoever other than the fact that he was drunk? Tell me more about that!"

Sure, coming to terms with and processing childhood struggles is a key component in therapy, and asking questions certainly helps with this process, but, just as important, is the step of examining the empowering moments in one's life. This is vital to de-Velcroing your mind! And remember, if you are going to complain about your parents, or any other significant adult figures from your childhood, and bitch about how they "screwed you up," you must also give them their rightful due for participating in the development of the phenomenal individual you are today!

De-Velcroing the mind is much more than identifying the positives and negatives of your life. Remember the Rat Race and how everyone is always rushing from home to work to the soccer fields? We must also learn to slow down for self-reflection. Healing and change begin with slowing down and sorting out the contents of your mind. Many well-known behavioral psychologists, like Dr. Michael Yapko, for example, stress the importance of "compartmentalizing." Picture this now—all the stuff in your head is stuck together in that Velcro ball, but now it's time to file all the stuff so that you can call on it and retrieve it in a more orderly and controlled fashion. I heard Yapko speak one time about "opening doors and closing doors."

He illustrated: "Oh, now I'll look behind Door Number 1. I'll open it and sit with and process that moment when I was thirteen years old and got my first kiss from Mary Clark behind the school bus. My heart almost exploded! Now I can shut Door Number 1 and open Door Number 2. Let me sit with that moment two weeks later, when I caught Mary kissing my best friend, Billy, behind the bus. Now my heart was crushed!"

It is a great visual image, this opening and closing of doors. And this picture of separation and understanding is what Dr. Schwartz was also explaining so many years ago. De-Velcroing the mind is very similar to compartmentalizing. How about that! A psychoanalyst and a behaviorist pretty much talking about the same thing!

Of course, one can compartmentalize into a satisfying state of denial. "I'll just shove that into a nice, neat drawer in my head and never open it again." But even if no one else knows about the drawer, I do, and it will eat at me and fester until I deal with what's in the drawer I won't open because it's too painful to face.

Let's get back to Dr. Schwartz's description of that Velcro ball. It's not just any old ball. It's not a piece of paper crumpled into a paper ball. It's not a snowball that can break apart in an instant or just melt away when the temperature rises. And it's not a water balloon that suddenly goes *POP* when it hits a sharp object. The reason it's called a Velcro ball is that everything in it is stuck together and hard to pull apart. Pulling this ball apart requires supreme effort. You must work at it very hard in order to force the pieces to separate. Worse, even if you are determined to eventually accomplish that great goal, you'd better watch out, because if the pieces separate but remain close enough together, the Velcro may snag them and smush

71

them all back together again. Sadly, after all that work of pulling and separating the many pieces of your life, you could find yourself right back where you started from!

Giving Yourself Room is all about this ability and willingness to de-Velcro the mind. Self-exploration and personal growth take time and patience. Key to understanding this process of de-Velcroing is not just recognizing the bad stuff and being willing to deal with it, but also appreciating the good stuff in life by creating separation. By Creating Space and allowing for separation, your mind Gives Room for clarity. It is this clarity that opens our eyes to the wonders of life and offers opportunities to develop creative solutions for the problems that trouble us. You must also learn to step out of the Rat Race to appreciate the good stuff. It's not enough to just acknowledge your gifts, or your strengths, or your uniqueness. It's an absolute necessity that you Give Yourself Room to embrace who you really are and let it be known that you are an extraordinary individual. Wave that flag of appropriate self-love! Wave it high!

Often our Velcro ball is packed with interconnected items that make us feel great about ourselves, as well as items that make us feel bad about ourselves. Giving Room offers a vehicle for reaching a point at which we recognize and accept the bad in our lives, set it aside, and choose to embrace what makes us feel good about ourselves. This process can Give a Person Room to break cycles of denial.

SEEING LIFE AS A CONTINUUM:
MOVING TOWARD "HEALTHY SELFISHNESS"

Have you ever noticed the intensity that some people display when it comes to liking or disliking another person? For many of us, these feelings can be so black and white. Sue, a forty-year-old client of mine, was screaming the other day, "I absolutely hate my brother! I cannot believe he was so selfish not to call me yesterday when I know our mother told him my cat was sick!" But just three weeks before, Sue was talking about how her brother spent the entire weekend working on her car. When I challenge Sue about the discrepancy, she shrugs it off and defends her righteous stance. "Oh, the only reason he was working on my car is because he loves my brownies and he knew I would give in and make them. He doesn't care two shits about me! He just knows I'm The Great Brownie Baker!"

And then there is the brilliant sixty-one-year-old carpenter whom I've been treating for about a year. He is known in the community as one of the most talented guys, working with his hands and building custom homes. He came to see me because he had "low self-esteem and trouble holding onto relationships." Over and over, he described intimate relationships that ended abruptly with him "being betrayed" or getting figuratively "slapped in the face." He said to me the other day with such passion, "I don't understand it! My whole life people have ripped my heart out. Why is it that I am so good at building things, except when it comes to relationships?!"

Julie, a sixteen-year-old sophomore in high school, who lost her virginity when she was in the eighth grade, struggles with another aspect of judging and evaluating others. Although we are starting to crack the fixed, interrelational pattern Julie has played out for several years, the script is hard to change. She meets a boy and talks about all of his wonderful traits. "Dr. Castro, you don't understand; this guy is different. He is so good to me! He pays attention to me and says I'm the most beautiful girl in the world!" Julie throws herself at the guy by exhibiting promiscuous behavior and buying him extravagant presents. Eventually her heart is broken when this "most wonderful boy in the world" abruptly dumps her after they have had sex or after a holiday during which she showered him with gifts that she bought with her hard-earned babysitting money. Slowing down and processing this dynamic for Julie is so difficult. As a teenager, she understandably struggles with wanting to be liked, but the block in Julie's mind, preventing her from grasping the reality that she is being taken advantage of, is tremendously powerful. Her mind immediately gravitates toward the next guy on the dating list.

With many of my clients, I often focus on "seeing life as a continuum." And one of the most fundamental and helpful questions I can ask myself when treating a client is: Where does this person fall along the narcissist-masochist continuum? A narcissist is a person who looks out for *only* his or her own needs and is absolutely not interested in the needs of others. It is all about self-gratification and ego strokes. It is all about "What have you done for me lately?" There is little or no empathy. At the other end of this continuum is the masochist. My own definition of a masochist is an individual whose calling in life is to tend to the needs of others. Ostensibly, they care *only* about the needs of others and frequently neglect their own needs in order to respond to those of others. You probably know some people who match the descriptions of narcissist or masochist.

At one extreme end of the continuum is the self-absorbed narcissist, and at the other extreme is the self-sacrificing masochist. Now here's the question: Which one is healthier? Is it the person who occupies the most extreme place of self-absorption or is it the giver at the farthest extreme of self-sacrifice? The answer: NEITHER! Perhaps you are asking, why is it so bad to want to help others? Are you telling me Mother Teresa and Gandhi were emotionally unhealthy?

The bottom line is, "Yes, it is *very* unhealthy to always be giving and attending to the needs of others." This behavior is unhealthy because it is absolutely impossible to please and help others all the time and still have space to Give Yourself Room to meet your own needs. You just can't live a happy or balanced life at either extreme of this continuum.

Consider, for example, Julie, our sixteen-year-old who puts all her time and energy into pleasing her boyfriend. Night and day, she obsesses about him. The thoughts are constant and almost impossible to shake. Over and over, she replays her last conversation with Mr. Wonderful. All the decisions she makes have the common goal of pleasing and winning the affection of the Love of Her Life. She picks up as many babysitting jobs as possible in order to buy him gifts. This work schedule takes away from her studies, leading to her failing two classes and having to attend summer school. It's not that Julie doesn't have the intellect to perform well in school. Rather, because she doesn't have the self-esteem and respect for herself to Give Room to her own needs, she doesn't allow enough time for herself or her studies. As for her boyfriend's libidinous needs, Julie knows both intellectually and morally that it's not wise to have sex at her age. But the superficial lies and promises from her boyfriend ("You are the most beautiful girl I've ever met" and "What do you think the names of our kids should be?") fill her fragile self-esteem cup just enough for Julie to give in and compromise herself.

Another reason it is so unhealthy to be at either extreme of the narcissist-masochist continuum is that the self-absorbed narcissist attracts the self-sacrificing masochist and vice versa. The "caring one" keeps giving and giving and giving, while the "egotistical one" keeps taking and taking and taking. Theoretically, the relationship should work because these two people complement each other. However, both the masochist and the narcissist share one fatal flaw that precludes any kind of solid or healthy relationship. They both lack self-esteem. Both rely on others in their own unique ways to attain a sense of their own worth. After a while, the masochist just gets tired of giving and giving, tired of being abused, tired of being disrespected. The heavy weight of the narcissist's expectations and lack of gratitude beat him down until he becomes depressed and resentful.

Like the rush from a stiff drink, the narcissist's feeling of accomplishment and gratification from getting what he wants are short-lived and superficial. The omnipotent feelings eventually wear off. And although this self-inflated individual would deny it, the reality is that, for all his grandiosity, he often feels shallow and sad. During quiet times, moments of despair and "Dark Nights of the Soul" invade his being. He feels like a thin shell that could crumble into thousands of pieces at any moment.

But the narcissist is resilient and eventually bounces back. He buries the feelings of desolation (he hides them in that convenient drawer he never opens), lifts his chin, and plows through life alone, superficially satisfied with a smile on his face. This pattern of happy, righteous selfishness followed by isolated emptiness becomes more extreme, more severe. Therefore, when the sad and lonely times have temporarily abated and the narcissist's omnipotent defenses are back in full gear, the masochist must give that much more to satisfy the narcissist. This "narcissistic supply" (as it is called) is the lifeblood of any card-carrying narcissist. Stick out your neck to "help" him, and like any good vampire, he will suck you dry! Now the masochist is really taking the hit, figuratively and, at times, literally.

The key to change when it comes to the narcissist-masochist continuum is to Give Yourself Room to move toward the middle. And what's in the middle? In the middle of this continuum is what I call "healthy selfishness," the free-flowing combination of believing in oneself and looking after one's own needs, yet still possessing the empathic qualities to be kind and humble. As a therapist, I will push the masochist to focus on his or her needs. Often, this is an extremely difficult chore for the masochist. He has spent his entire life listening and very carefully catering to the needs of others, and his behavior is dictated by the emotional pull he feels to please others and to their response, which shows him that he is succeeding. Consciously understanding, evaluating, and responding to his own needs aren't even on the radar screen. Likewise, empathizing with others is absolutely foreign territory to the narcissist—definitely off his radar screen. Other people don't show up there because, unlike himself, whom he can know and feel and care about, other people are simply abstractions to him. They are objects, like appliances, there to serve him, but he doesn't need them to feel better about himself. Neither the narcissist nor the masochist is likely to choose change readily. The masochist, however, is generally much better at identifying and acknowledging his problem. The narcissist seldom catches on that something is "not quite right" about himself—soul searching is not on his radar screen either.

To me, the realities in life are gray. Perhaps you're surprised to read this from a psychologist. So many people think we therapists *really do have all the answers* but we're mysteriously hiding them for the right time when we can pull them out of our hat, like a magician. But rarely do I see things as black and white. Therefore, I consider even the smallest of movements toward the absolute middle, toward the subtle shades of healthy selfishness, as positive growth. For example, if I can assist the narcissist even slightly, and even for only a few minutes, to listen to and take an interest in the needs of his wife— well, to me that's wonderful and positive change! And even if the masochist fights off the burning feeling in his gut just one time and voices his own need, to me, it is time for celebration! Remember, Giving Room is a process. It is a process of taking chances and taking steps. The chances may not be momentous at first and the steps may be small and tentative, but it is movement in a healthier direction.

Another approach I often take, particularly with the self-sacrificing masochist, is to point out assertively that, in reality, he is being selfish (unhealthily selfish, that is) in his extreme way of interacting with the world. He is focusing way too much on himself. Think about this for a moment. The masochist reads into things, assumes things as they relate only to him. In the therapy room, I hear comments from masochists like "That look in my boss's eye told me he was very upset with MY performance." Or, "Just imagine what my boyfriend would think if I told him that I really hate it when he smokes in my house; boy, would he be annoyed with ME." Or, "It is my obligation in my family to always give money when my mother or sister needs it; imagine what they would think of ME if I didn't!"

When these self-focused comments start flowing, I latch onto the pattern and pounce like a hungry Nittany Lion (Penn State's mascot!) on his prey. I pull my chair forward, look my client dead in the eyes, and say sternly, "Maybe it's not all about YOU!"

This confuses the masochist. "You don't get it, Dr. Castro," the client will say, "I am the one thinking about everyone else's needs. I am a giver, not a taker! Don't you get it?"

I get it. And it is at this point in our session that I begin the task of unearthing in these clients the selfish foundation of their feelings, thoughts, and behaviors. Consider the statement again: "What is that person thinking of ME?" And, "That stern look in my boss's eyes is clearly ALL about how he sees and evaluates ME." Again, "Can you imagine what my boyfriend would think of ME if I actually told him to cut out the smoking indoors?!" And finally, "My family members' financial woes rightfully fall on MY shoulders. It is MY duty to alleviate them!" In one way or another, these individuals are proclaiming, "It is all about me! I am in the middle, front, and center of attention, and the world and all the people in it revolve around me."

When working with these self-involved patients from the extreme ends of the narcissist-masochist continuum, a primary objective in treatment is for them to reach an understanding of how they contribute to the difficulties in their relationships. I want these folks to gain insight into the dynamic of how living at either extreme is not healthy for themselves or others. A light bulb needs to go on in the patient's mind, exposing the lie of living for another or completely satisfying that individual's needs. I'm happy when my patients experience an "A ha!" moment. This is the point in our therapy at which the patient grasps the wisdom that we psychotherapists are trained to provide. In the case of the masochist, the "A ha!" moment brings understanding that it is unrealistic to think there will be a healthy level of intimacy in relationships if one considers only his own needs. I try to show my patients that it is not all about THEM.

It is imperative that the masochist be able to verbalize (even if haltingly or somewhat incoherently) the part that he or she plays in the dysfunctional relationship. Being able to actually verbalize her complicity is key to making real positive change. Like the entranced bingo player who, upon hearing the winning number, awakens from his stupor and yells, "Bingo!" my patient proclaims, "Yes! I see, Dr. Castro, that when I am constantly doing things for my son it benefits me and actually prevents my son from learning responsibility. It's mainly about *me* not feeling as anxious! It's really not about him!"

The narcissist must create an opening in his self-centered fortress to let in some light. This will allow him to Give Himself Room to verbalize the true needs of others in his life. After almost two years in therapy, Bob has gained a modicum of trust in me. Bob is Mr. Powerful, an *I'll-do-what-I-want-when-I-want* father and husband. In fact, the reason Bob entered therapy in the first place was because his high-and-mighty stance had pushed people away, leaving him depressed and alone.

I asked, "Bob, what do you think it meant when your wife and your three kids were all crying Christmas morning? Why were they all crying, Bob?"

All-powerful Bob tries to fight off my direct blow. "What the hell do they care if I wasn't home Christmas morning? They still had their presents to open!"

Then silence descends in the therapy room for a good two minutes. Bob's glowering eyes pierce mine. He doesn't blink. I don't either. Finally, his head drops into his hands and he appears to be fighting tears. His voice trembles—he's experiencing the first fissure in his fortress. Finally he says, "The look in their eyes. Complete sadness." His words are few. But at least now his words exist! For years, these words were missing, but now I have heard them. More important, Bob has heard them. What Gave Bob Room to recognize and feel the sadness of his family was his willingness (although it took many years) to trust me and allow me to help him confront these issues.

THE SCRIPT

When people Give Themselves Room to be aware of their place along the narcissist-masochist continuum, it is a major step toward personal growth. But now these patients need new tools; they need a new script. For years they've trained themselves in how to react to every life situation, every problem, every confrontation as a narcissist or a masochist. Now that they have allowed themselves to see that little fissure in the emotional walls of their fortress and see that it is not all about them, they don't know what to say or how to react to life's "stuff." They are quite literally confused about how they feel. This is all new to them. They have never felt like this before, and it can be quite overwhelming. They need help. These patients are now growing; they are full of knowledge but have yet to do the new verbal dance of interacting with others in a "healthily selfish" manner. It's my job to help them move to the middle of the spectrum and teach them a new language that promotes balance on this continuum. Often, I will use the modeling approach—literally give them the script and instruct them to "say what I say" or to simply "repeat after me." This modeling approach can be very helpful in guiding the client toward healthier interactions with others and a higher level of self-esteem. At times, clients have even pulled out paper and pen and started to transcribe my words as they begin to learn a new way of relating.

You may be thinking, *This seems rather superficial for the patient to be robotically repeating and writing down exactly what you say! It doesn't Give Room for the client to think on his own!*

I totally disagree! I love it when a patient reaches for the pad of paper in my office and says, "Now hold on, Dr. Castro. What was that you just said? I want to write this down." It communicates to me that my patient is actively engaged in therapy. They are Giving Themselves Room to step forward (not backward) into possibly doing something different in life. Yes, I am giving them the words, but in essence they are taking charge! They want the words! Being proactive in seeking and then following the lead of experts is a key ingredient to Giving Yourself Room.

My favorite "script story" is about Ben, a ten-year-old fifth-grader whose parents brought him to therapy because he was struggling with a bully at school. Ben is the coolest kid, with straight, long blond hair and an adorable smile. He is very engaging, highly intelligent, and surprisingly humble for a child his age. When we chat, he reminds me of a caring old grandpa—Ben is wise beyond his years. However, he also has a serious problem. At times, Ben is too nice, and the class bully, Alec, preys on him.

Through our discussions, Ben has done a great job of

coming up with ways to confront Alec's abuse in a healthy, mature way. For example, when Alec intentionally tripped Ben on the playground, Ben, in an authoritative yet still respectful tone, faced Alec sternly and said, "Stop picking on me and stop tripping me. I don't think it's funny. I don't like it and it needs to stop!" When Alec called Ben names in front of all their peers or taped a sign to the back of Ben's shirt that read, "I'm Mr. Stupid!" Ben tried the tactic of ignoring Alec while telling himself, "Ben, you are a better person than he is. . . . Just let it go." Ben even tried befriending Alec by inviting him over after school. However, Alec laughed at Ben. "Why would I want to go to Mr. Stupid's house?" Nothing seemed to be working, and Alec's bullying continued.

Unfortunately, after a few months in therapy, Ben's emotional health was getting worse, not better. He obsessed about what Alec would say or do to him the next day. His worry made it difficult for him to fall asleep, and he often woke up in the morning in a state of anxiety, complaining about his upset stomach, clearly a psychosomatic symptom from all the nervousness. Also, Ben started exhibiting defiant behavior at home toward his parents. This behavior was quite uncharacteristic of loveable and loving Ben.

As Ben's anxiety rose, so did my anger. Do therapists get angry over their patients' circumstances? Damn right we do. I was furious that this kid was bullying my patient, causing him such great emotional distress. I was angry with the teacher as well for not taking Ben's complaints seriously. Ben had approached his teacher on several occasions, detailing this bully's actions, but the teacher downplayed the attacks. Condescendingly, she said, "Now, Ben, you just need to try to get along with Alec or simply stay away from him!"

It was time to give Ben a script. I began, "Ben, I need you to do me a favor." (Ben is such a pleaser, I knew I would get his full attention if I started off asking him for a favor.) "Ben, the next time Alec verbally or physically harasses you, I need you to stop what you're doing and immediately go to Mr. Jones's (the principal) office. If you're in class, you don't even have to ask to be excused. Just walk out and go to his office."

Ben listened attentively and nodded. "Okay, I can do that."

I continued. "And Ben, here's what I need you to say to Mr. Jones. . . ."

The following week Ben strolled into my office wearing a big smile. "Hi, Dr. Castro!"

We began chatting, and I casually asked Ben, "So has Alec been giving you any trouble lately?" Because Ben is such a nice kid, I assumed he would just keep trying to avoid Alec and hopefully fly under the "Alec radar screen" for the final five weeks of school. Besides, I knew that for Ben to follow my script would mean directly entering into a confrontational and scary situation by going to the principal's office. In the past, Ben had tried to avoid discussing the topic with me and clearly downplayed the agony he was experiencing. It was the updates from his mom that really gave me a true picture of the pain he was feeling over the past couple of months.

Confidently, Ben answered, "Yes, Dr. Castro, a situation happened with Alec."

Concerned, I quickly asked, "What happened, Ben? Was he teasing you again?"

Ben told the story. It was brilliant! "Well, Dr. Castro, I was sitting in math class and Alec was sitting right behind me and he smacked me with a rubber band paper wad in the back of my neck. I immediately got up. I asked to be excused to go to the bathroom. I didn't feel comfortable breaking the teacher's rule by not asking to be excused. Then I walked straight into Mr. Jones's office and said to him, 'Sir, I need to talk to you.'"

My heart was racing as I nodded at Ben encouragingly.

He continued. "So I said to Mr. Jones, 'Mr. Jones, my psychologist, Dr. Tony Castro (I love it that Ben called me Tony. No one calls me Tony except old professors from graduate school and my good friend Mark Arnett!), told me the next time Alec hurts me I should walk immediately into your office and tell you. A few minutes ago Alec shot me with a rubber band paper wad on the back of my neck. So that's why I'm in your office, because Dr. Tony Castro told me to go to you, and here's the welt on the back of my neck.'"

According to Ben, the angry look on Mr. Jones's face was priceless! I thought *I* was mad at the way Ben was being treated by Alec, but Mr. Jones was absolutely furious! In all my years as a psychologist, I had never heard of a principal coming down so hard on a kid for bullying as Mr. Jones did that day. Alec's parents were immediately summoned to the school. Their son was suspended for several weeks, he lost all school privileges for the rest of the year, and Alec was required to write a three-page letter apologizing to Ben and his parents for the abusive behavior. Sure, most heads of schools talk a good game about disciplining bullies, particularly after the Columbine shootings of April 1999, but the reality is that many administrators just don't want to make waves. Besides Mr. Jones's need to protect the school's reputation (he knows I'm still paying attention), he also wants to create a safe school environment. The key to this story, though, was Ben. He made it clear that there was a problem and asserted himself in a new way. And he could do this because he "followed the script."

CREATING SPACE FOR HAPPINESS

Because Ben precisely followed my instructions, even though doing so was outside of his comfort zone, healthy behavior change occurred and Ben felt empowered. After he'd followed the script and people around him reacted, his symptoms decreased. Ben was able to sleep soundly through the night, his obsessive thinking drastically decreased, and the stomachaches magically disappeared. By following the script, Ben got a taste of what it's like for a ten-year-old to embrace a moment of healthy selfishness! As Ben's case illustrates, giving a client a script can be a very helpful tool. These step-by-step instructions explaining what to say and how to behave give comfort and confidence to clients and help them to fight off the overwhelmingly anxious feelings that prevent them from thinking clearly. The script allows them to Give Themselves Room to try a new approach, confront a problem, or reach out in a way they never had before. When one has a script to follow, the worry that would distort healthy thinking is significantly reduced. Furthermore, clients can adapt the script to other situations; they need not always be given a new script to follow when a different situation arises.

PERRY MASON MODEL

I used to giggle with excitement as a kid, watching the TV attorney nonchalantly asking his defendant question after question and then, suddenly, the case would be solved! It amazed me how Mr. Mason used a series of questions to solve his cases. Today, I deal with real life, and although it's filled with real drama and real action, I have borrowed Perry Mason's techniques to assist some of my own patients. Those who require a more subtle approach than following a detailed script that tells them exactly what to do are more comfortable with a script in the form of questions. Offering the script as a series of questions helps lead the individual down a new road of thinking. Unlike the direct approach of "do what I say," which may restrict room for discussion, delivering the script in question format Gives Room to the client to enter into a discussion about the topic at hand. Furthermore, this approach hands over a good deal of control to the patient. If the patient does not find the script helpful, she has the option of pushing it aside. If she is not ready to hear the new script (that is, if her defenses are still too strong), my question is ultimately heard as a slight misfire, and she maneuvers around it without incident. Soliciting the listener's ideas through questioning is a much softer and more palatable way to deliver a script than telling her what to do. My "Perry Mason model" of leading a person via questions also has the advantage of helping me with the timing of my comments. Regardless of whether the patient engages or negates the question, her response helps me know how much I can nudge her in a new direction.

Annie, an attractive thirty-year-old woman whom I have been treating for three years, offers a great example of the "dance" a therapist and patient may engage in during self-discovery. Annie pushes away her feelings of loneliness, sadness, and fear by getting annoyed with the world's inability to be "good enough." Name any person in Annie's life—family member, employer, partner, neighbor, customer service representative—and Annie will inevitably zero in on that person's faults. However, at times Annie will jump to the other side of the fence and glorify that same person, in effect wearing blinders to any negatives. I am constantly trying to push Annie

87

toward the middle, through questions, no matter what end of the spectrum she is at—all positive or all negative.

I present the first question. Annie is fixated on her wonderful new partner, Karl, and often makes comments such as, "We just seem to have this connection" or "We seem to flow so well together." I say, "You guys have been dating for a couple of months and it seems clear that you have two major concerns about the relationship. First, it's obvious that you are concerned about the age issue (Karl is nineteen), and second, the money issue (Karl's not working or going to school and has no money; Annie makes six figures). What do you imagine Karl would say if you brought up these issues?"

My question provides Annie with a loose script of how to tackle difficult issues in the early stages of a healthy romantic relationship. Not surprisingly, Annie completely ignores my question. Furthermore, she rudely interrupts me in the middle of a question: "Anthony, what's especially interesting about Karl is that just the other day . . ."

I have learned over time when these interruptions occur to sternly remark, "I'm not finished, Annie" and immediately finish my question. Occasionally, my assertive stance will startle her enough to hear some of what I'm saying. Even so, Annie's negation of my question is good information for me. It communicates to me that she is not ready to engage in a conversation about Giving Room to doing something uncomfortably different: confronting her partner about sensitive issues.

The good news about introducing a new script (in question form or not) is that it can be used at a later date, even if Annie ignores it the first time. On several occasions throughout our work together, she has discounted my words or fired off a piercing verbal barb when I've pushed her to think about a new script, a new way to interact and Give Herself Room. I am left, at times, feeling that Annie just doesn't get what I'm trying to communicate to her. To my pleasant surprise, however, she may reference the script two months later! Like creating a spring garden, where planting seeds doesn't produce an abundant harvest overnight, the therapist's new script needs time to sink in with the patient in order to result in growth.

In sum, life is a lonely place for those who live at either extreme of the narcissist-masochist continuum. This self-involved way of relating leaves little room for deep relationships. Too often, not being in the balanced middle moves people to feel resentful or quasi-omnipotent, and these unhealthy feelings become more severe if they do not Give Themselves Room to change. One key to personal growth is to Give Yourself Room to develop healthy selfishness. It is my job as a therapist to explain to clients that they have to understand why it is perfectly fine to possess a healthy sense of selfishness. This will lead to Giving Room. When we veer toward either extreme along the selfish-selfless continuum, our focus is one-sided; too focused on ourselves while ignoring the contribution of others in the relationship. We must verbalize our role in these unhealthy relationships. By articulating and understanding our placement along the narcissist-masochist continuum, we Give Ourselves Room for healthier communication and stronger, lasting intimacy in all relationships.

CREATING SPACE FOR HAPPINESS

HOLLY'S STORY: "I AM WATCHING YOU"

Caroling, caroling through the town. Christmas bells are ringing! Joy and cheer filled the air as Eydie Gorme's classic voice wafted through eight-year-old Emily Peterson's home. Outside, the snow streamed down on this wintry December evening. Three inches had already fallen in two hours, and by morning's end, a total of a foot and a half would be on the ground. Inside, the Petersons' home was in full Christmas regalia. At twenty-two feet, the "cathedral pine" (as the family jokingly called it) was decked in silver and gold ribbons, colored lights, and heirloom ornaments. Hanging from the mantel of the blazing hearth were the stockings of all five family members: Mom, Dad, Emily, and her two sisters. Garlands with plastic red berries weaved through every room. A large mistletoe hung in the foyer. That familiar holiday aroma of burning pinewood and cinnamon cider simmering on the stove filled the air. Ah, Christmas!

When the party first began, the emotions of the twenty-plus kids exploded like firecrackers as they raced through every room in the house. Quickly, these youngsters were relegated to the basement play area; they needed to be limited to destroying only the downstairs. But the basement was a kid's paradise, offering video games, pool table, jukebox, LEGOs, air hockey, trunks of clothes for dress-up games, and hundreds of board games. Their yelling and laughing continued, but the high-pitched screeches were mercifully muffled behind the closed door. Every half hour or so, a few of the kids would approach the top few stairs, only to be directed back down by Mrs. Peterson. As the eggnog and brandy began to flow, the parents breathed a sigh of relief and relaxed.

Holly wasn't interested in joining in with the kids. She stayed upstairs. Mrs. Peterson was well aware of Holly's separation from the other kids and she allowed it, for she was aware that Holly was no ordinary child. Whenever Holly made a request, Mrs. Peterson's answer was always, "Of course, sweetie." Holly and Emily had been friends for the past twenty-two months. They'd become classmates midway through the second grade, when Holly moved to town and settled in the subsidized apartment complex across from school. Also, Katie and Emily's sister Chloe became friends when they entered kindergarten in the fall. For the past several months, Holly and Katie had spent much time at the Petersons', frequently coming over after school and not leaving until after dinner. On the weekends, the girls usually spent the night at least once. It didn't take Emily's mother long to sense the lack of consistent parenting in the lives of these two girls. Mrs. Peterson was a loving caregiver, determined to share some comfort and love with the Smith girls.

The first time Holly and Katie joined them for supper, Mrs. Peterson was floored. It wasn't that the two girls were so well behaved that shocked Emily's mother. Nor was it their proper table manners and the fact that they always said, "Please" and "Thank you." What most caught Mrs. Peterson's attention was the obvious "mother-daughter" relationship between Holly and Katie. When Katie was out of juice, she'd turn to her sister and say, "Holly, may I please have a little more juice?"

Holly would give her sister an approving look and say, "You're showing some very good manners, Katie. But now I want you to ask Mrs. Peterson if it's okay to have some more juice."

91

Similarly, when Chloe and Katie finished their meals, both would jump up and ask to be excused, Chloe turning to her mom and Katie to Holly. Sure, Holly was only a nine-year-old child, but Mrs. Peterson often felt she was talking to an adult when interacting with Holly.

On this snowy, festive night, Mrs. Peterson's focus now turned to the adults. Like a watchful bear tending to her cubs, she scanned the party, determined to make everyone's evening enjoyable. That's when her eye caught Holly in the back corner of the room, inconspicuously flipping through her spiral notepad. Mrs. Peterson's eyes brightened as she approached the little girl. "Hi, sweetie."

Holly shoved the notepad into her back pocket. "Oh, hello, Mrs. Peterson. What a lovely party you're hosting this evening. Thank you again for inviting my family. My mother wanted me to tell you she was saddened she couldn't make it."

Warmly, Mrs. Peterson hugged Holly's shoulder. "Holly, you know you folks are always welcome in my home." Holly leaned in to Mrs. Peterson's side, acknowledging the caring words. With enthusiasm, Mrs. Peterson turned to Holly, placing her hands on Holly's shoulders and squatting down to make eye contact with her. "Okay, Holly. You've had some time to check out the list. So whom are you thinking of?"

A week earlier, Holly had approached Mrs. Peterson about a "personal project" she wanted to complete. Holly knew there would be many prominent adults at the Petersons' holiday party and felt it would be a wonderful forum to learn about these individuals. She had asked Mrs. Peterson if it would be okay to interview a few of the adults about their professions. Mrs. Peterson was ecstatic. "What a wonderful idea, honey! I know it would be great fun for them. And what a wonderful learning experience for you!" Now that the night of the party had arrived, it was decision time. "I'm assuming you want to talk to Dr. Nichols or Dr. Trundel? Or maybe both? Anyone else from the list you're thinking of?"

Holly had not only asked Mrs. Peterson for the names and professions of the guests but had also requested that Mrs. Peterson give a physical description to her. This allowed her to know within the first five minutes of the party who everyone was. She had spent the beginning of the party observing and jotting down notes about her top five individuals and now had narrowed it down to two. She said, "Well, yes, Mrs. Peterson. First I would like to spend some time with Dr. Trundel. I'm very impressed and excited about talking to a pediatric cardiovascular surgeon. Also, I was thinking Mrs. Balman would be fun to talk to. I've never met a college professor before."

Mrs. Peterson nodded. "I'll be back in five minutes after I talk to both of them."

Dr. Trundel was an attractive middle-aged woman who didn't bother wearing makeup to enhance her beauty. Her long, dirty-blonde hair was pulled back and, combined with her slender frame and green eyes, made her physical appearance striking. Even more than her looks, though, Holly was impressed by Dr. Trundel's radiant confidence as she worked the room at the party. The doctor did not jump around like a butterfly hoping to talk to everyone. Nor did she devote all of her time to just one long conversation. She balanced her interactions with three or four people.

"Dr. Trundel, I would like to introduce you to Holly Smith. As I mentioned to you, Holly wants to be a doctor someday and would love to interview you for a few minutes about what it's like to be an MD." And suddenly the transformation began: All at once, Holly's hyperfocus zeroed in as she opened her mind's mental notepad and began scribbling bullet point after bullet point. Now that Holly was centered in her own little world, the rest of the party was far in the distance. Holly's concentration on Dr. Trundel was almost trance-like, yet purposeful.

Dr. Trundel sat on the sofa next to the little girl. "Hello, Holly, it's nice to meet you." Holly's mind began to race; she could hear her own heartbeat. Bullet point one: *Makes clear yet warm eye contact.* Bullet point two: *Hand is extended and tilted at a thirty-two-degree angle. Handshake firm but not uncomfortable. Hand temperature warm but not sweaty.* Bullet point three: *Tone of voice communicates a friendly interest, yet is not overly excited.*

Shaking hands, Holly responded, "It's very nice to meet you as well, Dr. Trundel. Thanks for spending some time with me."

For the next twenty minutes, Dr. Trundel answered Holly's questions about being a doctor: "What got you interested in medicine?" "What is the MCAT exam really like?" "What made you decide on pediatric cardiology as opposed to another discipline?" "Can you tell me about the training process in medical school?" Dr. Trundel answered many questions in the same way. Bullet point fifteen: *Frequently begins answer with "That's a very good question." Makes the other person feel appreciated.* Impressed by Holly's inquisitive questions, the doctor answered her inquiries thoroughly. Bullet point twenty-one: *Structures her responses by immediately answering the question, then moves into a more comprehensive description of the topic.*

Only Holly actually knew that the questions she asked Dr. Trundel were decoys strategically staged to Give Holly Room to learn—and one day to emulate the responses. Both Mrs. Peterson and Dr. Trundel were unaware of Holly's real objective. To them, Holly looked excited, attentive, and somewhat nervous. Just a rather mature nine-year-old talking to a real-life surgeon. But inside her little body, Holly was a detective, a seasoned investigator smoothly interrogating her idol in a non-confrontational manner. These adults had no idea Holly's mind was giggling, "I'm watching you!" Holly already knew about "how to become a doctor." The questioning was needed to free her mind to gather the real stuff she was looking for. She had mapped out her questions, knowing they would buy her approximately one half hour of time.

Holly had become a pro at observing adults. Watching and learning were the "daily tasks" she assigned herself every morning. Holly would rise from bed and say out loud, "So who am I watching today?" While many of the kids were running around the playground during recess, Holly would likely be sitting on the sidewalk, occasionally glancing over at the volunteer adult monitor. She would watch, and the bullet points would start racing through her head. To Holly, *watching* was much more beneficial than listening. Listening drew upon the communicator's content, or lack thereof. Holly wasn't short on content. Her mind was like a sponge when it came to content. She knew how to get book knowledge without anyone else's help. Intuitively, she was aware she needed more to survive in life.

Holly used all environments as training ground. For example, to Holly, "Parents' Week" felt like what other kids described as Christmas morning. That's the week the kids would bring their moms or dads to school and have them discuss their professions. The kids would ask questions like "What's it like being a fireman?" or "Do you have to be good at math to become an accountant?" Holly wouldn't pay much attention to their words. She would watch and learn as their bodies and gestures did the teaching.

Dr. Trundel concluded, "Well, Holly, I really enjoyed talking with you this evening." Bullet point forty-two: *A warm smile: lips closed. Left hand softly rubs my back.*

"Likewise, Dr. Trundel," Holly agreed. "I really enjoyed talking to you too." Bullet point forty-three: *Eye contact is broken. Eyes start to glance around the room as she takes a sip of her white wine (half full), clearly an indication that she is ending the conversation.* Holly continued, "I won't keep you any longer, Dr. Trundel, but I just had one last quick question." Bullet point forty-four: *Her eyes quickly reconnect and communicate warmth.*

"Sure, Holly, what is it?" she asked.

"In the future, if I think of any more questions, would you mind if we met again? Because, you know, someday I really want to be just like you." Bullet point forty-five: *Communicates a feeling of connection by immediately dropping into a squatting position making eye contact. Both hands gently squeeze my arm.*

"You bet, Holly! I can't wait for your call!"

Holly whispers to herself as Dr. Trundel departs, "Neither can I, neither can I."

LISTEN TO YOUR GUT?

Business executives make hiring decisions based on a "gut feeling." Coaches use gut instincts when deciding which play to call at the crucial moment in a game. Parents have gut feelings about what mischief their children might be getting into. During certain overwhelming life events, has anyone ever told you, "What you really need to do is listen to your gut"? Then there's the perennial favorite: "Just follow your heart." I hear these two similar sayings frequently in my personal and professional life. There is a ton of advice, particularly in self-help books, that encourages people to "take the lead by going with what your gut tells you." I hear it everywhere. Parents encourage their kids to "do what feels right." Preachers passionately entreat us to "do what that small, still voice deep inside commands." Even psychologists will probe, "What do your feelings tell you?" All around, people are advising you to act according to how you feel.

Honestly, that facile wisdom of "go with what your gut tells you" scares the hell out of me! To me, leading a patient to "tell me what your heart says" is a surefire way to frustrate that person and strengthen the stronghold of resistance to change. I am inviting them to reinforce all the emotions and feelings that verify how they currently think about themselves. I want them to confront their gut, not to be ruled by it.

Not to digress too much, but this also leads to the topic of "can therapy hinder personal growth?" Can I actually damage a client by asking, "Just tell me how you feel?" I remember a professor in graduate school saying to me, "Anthony, I can't really think of anything you could say to a patient that would really hurt him, or cause him to regress. Certainly, there are thoughts that you can communicate, or advice you might give that really wouldn't help at all. But actually hurt the client? No, I don't see how you could hurt the person."

Sadly, I have learned over my years in practice that my professor was absolutely wrong! I don't want to imply that therapists are in such a controlling, almighty position that we act as puppeteers, dangling our vulnerable patient-puppets on strings, but the nature of the therapist-patient relationship creates a dynamic in which the therapist *is* an authority— someone to follow. As a therapist, I need to be very careful and understand that my words, even just one word, can have a huge impact on any of my clients. All too often therapists are clueless as to which words may impact their patients, both positively and negatively. Therefore, I would advise therapists to slow down and really question whether nonchalantly asking a patient, as he or she enters the office, "So how are you feeling today?" or "What does your gut tell you?" is beneficial to the therapeutic process.

Why would we want someone to listen to his or her gut? Often, it is that feeling in one's gut that keeps a person stuck! Do you think that Julie, the sixteen-year-old "giver" I described earlier in this chapter, would have changed her unhealthy choices if she just listened to her gut? Her boyfriend calls her cell phone at one in the morning: "Hey, baby, why don't you sneak out and crawl through my window. I miss you so much, baby; I really need to see you." It is Julie's mind, not her gut or heart, that calmly whispers, in a most proper British accent, "Now, Julie, you and I both know that leaving this house in the wee hours of the morning is only going to lead to trouble. You are a smart person, Julie. We both know that the only reason he's calling is because he wants to have sex. He's not interested in how your day has gone or in just cuddling tonight. Just like the five other times in the past two months, he wants to have sex with you and then he will be done with you. Once the sex is over, my dear Julie, he will be rude and mean, and you will be left feeling hurt and used." Suddenly, Julie's churning (and insecure) gut jumps in and elbows the mind smack in the face! Her mind drops from the fierce blow and is left cowering in the corner. At this point, trusty old gut forcibly grabs her by the collar and screams, "How many times have I told you, Julie? He loves you and wants to be with you forever. That leather jacket you got him for Christmas really clinched the deal! Because of that most wonderful gift, he now knows just how much you care—far more than anybody he's ever known or is likely to know! Yes, you are the one in his heart. You are The One! And see, having sex has always been a good thing! In so many ways you have showed him your love, and now he's feeling lonely for you and wants to show his love! So don't *think*; just *run*! Run to his house as fast as you can!"

For most people, their gut is far more compelling and confusing than their mind, particularly in adulthood. The gut is instinctual and impulsive. The gut is where all those intense, diverse feelings are embedded from infancy onward. However, during childhood we were able to "feel our feelings" in a more pure and deep way. Children have the ability to sit with a feeling in its unadulterated form much longer than adults. Not forever, of course. Children are also equipped with an arsenal of defenses that bury feelings in their truest form. Yet children can differentiate and articulate the array of feelings they experience more clearly than they can as adults. Little Jacob's voice quivers, "Oh, no! My parents are arguing again and it's getting really loud. It makes me so scared that they might get divorced." Eight-year-old Samantha's eyes well with tears as she phones her grandma to say, "Grandma, Rover didn't wake up this morning. Mommy says Rover is in Doggy Heaven but I miss him and I'm really sad! When are you coming over, Grandma? I need you!" And then there is my five-year-old daughter Zoe's favorite: "Daddy, I am so angry with you for not letting me have that Popsicle!" She grits her teeth and squeezes her fists. "Don't talk to me!" Most kids can sit with and verbalize their feelings much better than we adults.

As discussed earlier in the de-Velcroing section, these jumbled feelings residing in our gut are all stuck together. And because they are so enmeshed, so static, and so stuck, they are confusing and hard to understand. For example, when a mighty feeling, such as love, strikes one of my patients in the chest like a lightning bolt, he or she will often trip over their words when I ask about the new relationship. For example, remember my patient Annie and her new partner, Karl? I asked, "So Annie, what is it about this guy that drew you to him?"

Annie smiles, shakes her head, and shrugs her shoulders. "There is just this feeling of deep connection with him."

I inquire, "What do you mean by 'connection?'" She squirms like a kid who has finally been found during a game of hide-and-seek.

"You got me!" Annie remarks. "We just seem to be on the same wavelength."

It is vague phrases like these—"There is this feeling of connection" or "We are on the same wavelength"—that are sure signs that the person is focused on their gut or heart, and not their mind. My discussion with Annie continues, and by the end of the session I comment, "Annie, obviously you know better than I do, and I'm not in the relationship—you are (I love hedging my bets when confronting my clients. Clearly, I struggle at times with the fear that my patients may become angry at me for what I say and abandon me forever!), but doesn't this new relationship seem similar to previous relationships you have been in that led to lies and hurt?" Annie is an extremely bright woman. Her mind understands the dynamics. And she is insightful enough to intellectually recognize that this relationship likely won't last. But it is Annie's racing heart and the piercing feeling in her gut that keeps her locked in.

A fundamental rule we must follow when Giving Ourselves Room is not to *"listen* to our gut" but to *"delay* the feeling in our gut." Giving oneself time to just sit with an intense feeling— hate, passion, anger, love, and so on—is extremely therapeutic and often provides clarity to a given relationship or event. Yet, as we all know from experience, delaying the reaction to a powerful feeling is one of the hardest challenges in life. How often have you observed some middle-aged lunatic on the highway explode in an all-out rage because somebody unintentionally cut him off in the fast lane? How frequently have you witnessed a sibling or friend catering hand-and-foot to his wife, even though she is constantly verbally abusive to him? And how many events can you look back on from your own life and say, "Darn! If only I had stopped myself for a second or two and thought about the situation before just reacting to it! Rather than firing off that scathing e-mail, I wish I'd written a letter and put it in a drawer for a day or two while I cooled down!" Using time to our advantage by delaying a reaction when strong emotions arise is a crucial first step in successfully Giving Ourselves Room. We Give Ourselves Room to *experience* intense emotion rather than *acting* on it.

Joanne, a forty-three-year-old divorced mother of two, is a great example of how a methodical mind uses time to enrich and cultivate relationships in her professional life. But sometimes in her personal life, Joanne's impulsive, confused heart "rushes things," and she finds herself and her family in discord. A seasoned schoolteacher, Joanne has devoted the past twenty-two years to educating and coaching high school girls. She's taken her calling very seriously, at times obsessing about ways to improve as a teacher. Her passion for teaching and mentoring her students earned Joanne "Teacher of the Year" and "Coach of the Year" awards on several occasions. Her students adore her, her players admire her, and the school administrators feel blessed to have such a dedicated and contributing team player.

When it comes to her teaching world, Joanne enjoys a nice balance of listening to her mind and learning from her gut. At times, Joanne even plays the role of therapist for her students and players when they struggle emotionally. The empathy and counsel Joanne offers these kids is authentic and deeply felt. As warm as she is intelligent, Joanne is a helper and a healer. During staff meetings, Joanne frequently assumes a mediating role and is able to stay poised, hearing all sides of heated discussions. She weighs the arguments and responds with both warmth and wisdom. These spats between her colleagues can feel like an endless tennis match, Joanne tells me. Almost magically, Joanne simply clears her throat and eloquently mediates their arguments, no matter how petty or important. She speaks and the room listens. And when the timing is right, Joanne calmly and assertively speaks to her colleagues. She communicates her convictions concerning school issues, learning from her gut and always patient with feelings.

However, for Joanne, dealing with her sixteen-year-old son, Frankie, is a completely different story! According to the divorce decree signed years ago, Joanne is to spend every Sunday with Frankie. Joanne bought Frankie a cell phone so they could talk several times daily. Joanne and Frankie maintained their Sunday visits consistently for years, attending the morning church service, followed by an early lunch. At lunch, Joanne would get the weekly update. "Tell me, Frankie, what's going on at school?" "How are your friends?" "Are you thinking of trying out for the musical this year? You always loved the movie *Annie* when you were younger!" Frankie would give his mother what she craved. "Mom, you'll never believe how Jack and Terry got in trouble during science class! Oh, and wait till I tell you about my A in math!" Joanne soaked up the words. She really didn't care about content. She was focused on the exchange and the connection with her child.

The afternoon brought more bonding time as Frankie and Joanne engaged in a fun, interactive activity (going to the zoo, swimming at the pool, biking along the canal, etc.). They would chat about Frankie's dream of becoming a fighter pilot when he grew up. In the evening, Frankie would do his homework while Joanne picked up Chinese food. Their intimate, fun-filled day would end in laughter as the two snuggled up on the couch, chopsticks in hand, watching a double episode of *The Simpsons*. At bedtime, Joanne would turn out the lights and kiss Frankie on both cheeks and smile. Her heart would be full as she thought, *I love him and he loves me.*

Things started to change between Joanne and her son once Frankie became a teenager. Joanne's daily calls to her son were often ignored, and, like so many teenagers with their parents, Frankie's conversations with his mother were flat and short. Sundays had changed as well. Frankie now felt church was a drag, and his body language let this be known. No longer would he sing with joy and clap with the rest of the congregation. He clearly was not interested in worship. Their lunch rituals also annoyed Frankie. Ever so gently, as she did with her more sensitive students at school, Joanne would ask Frankie about his week. He would respond with one- or two-word answers. This frustrated and saddened Joanne. The rest of the day was just more of the same. He was disconnecting. As time went on, Frankie would try to bow out of the afternoon events and the sleepover at his mother's, opting to hang out with friends.

When Joanne first came to see me two years ago, she was deflated and angry. She described how she was calm and cool with her students but how the "new teenage Frankie" infuriated her. "I keep pushing to get more from him, asking him questions, even buying him things. But the more I push, the more he shuts down." As therapy progressed, Joanne was able to touch on and describe the wounded feelings in her gut when Frankie disengaged. She became capable of assigning words to her gut feelings: "I feel I am literally losing my breath when Frankie shuts down. It's like I'm drowning and I've got to fight for my life to stay alive! I feel that I've lost all control!" The relational pattern with her son was clear. The more Joanne grasped for more contact and interaction, the farther Frankie ran.

Joanne was a giver and a healer. Many of her students and players over the years longed for her words of wisdom. Frankie, however, wanted no part of them. Helping Joanne Give Room to herself and her son by not impulsively pushing the relationship was extremely difficult in the beginning. Her gut would yell, "Talk talk talk! Push push push!!" Yet her mind knew, *this getting in his face and ranting and raving just ain't working.* Joanne would rail, "I am not just going to ignore my son and let him do whatever he pleases! He needs to spend time with his mother! He needs to show me some respect and appreciation! Don't you think it's important to communicate with your kids, Dr. Know-It-All?" Joanne would, of course, apologize to me at our next session for her sarcastic jabs.

I explained to Joanne the importance of delaying the expression of feelings in her gut. "Sit with it for a while," I'd tell her. "Let the anger, resentment, and hurt rest for some time." I would not disagree with Joanne about her son's self-centeredness. "Yes, your son is being rude to his caring mother," and "You are right, Joanne. It does take two for a relationship to work. I couldn't agree more that you deserve better." Even though her son's behavior was inappropriate, I pushed Joanne to "fake it till you make it" by reacting to her son in a different way. I encouraged her to disregard how her gut was telling her to react and to do something different, to Give Herself Room to respond to Frankie in a different way.

"Fake it till I make it?!" she shot back in astonishment. "You have lost it, Dr. C. Don't you think it's about time we got that little shit into your office to talk some sense into him?"

I told Joanne that I would not see her son and that I thought he was a normal teenager. Frankie got good grades, didn't use drugs, and participated in healthy extracurricular activities. He had a good core group of friends and, yes, he was selfish and not interested in bonding with one of his parents. Seemed right in the healthy selfishness zone for a well-adjusted teenager! Sharing my own personal outlook on the matter, I told her, "I don't know, Joanne, but when my kids are teenagers, if their lives look like Frankie's, I'm going to be pretty happy!"

Slowly, Joanne began to back off. She would not indulge the reaction in her gut when she didn't get what she wanted from Frankie. For example, whenever she left Frankie a message on his cell phone and he didn't call back for several days, her heart hurt and she was angry. Her gut commanded, "Call him up and blast him! Tell him how hurt you are and how disrespectful he is!" Joanne worked hard to not react to these feelings. She started Giving Herself Room and pushed aside or even ignored the imperatives from her gut.

I would point to her and sternly say, "Joanne, the rule is you are not allowed to call him for three days once you've left a message. And when he does finally call, you must not talk about the message you left. Nor should you talk about how sad you are that he hasn't called in a while."

Finally, when Frankie returned the call, Joanne would follow my instructions and fake it. She began to notice that if she followed the script and pretended everything was fine, Frankie actually gave her more of the connection and words she so yearned for. She would be elated during her next therapy session. "I let the feelings go, and suddenly we were talking again!" Joanne was learning that the more she controlled the feelings in her gut and Gave Room to doing "something different," the more she'd get what she wanted. As time went on, Joanne was able to gain more understanding of why she reacted so differently to Frankie than she did to her kids at school. She learned that her anger and hurt were just a cover-up for the feelings of sadness and loss as she watched her one and only child transition into young adulthood. She mourned the loss of her little boy, as Frankie maneuvered through the separation from his mother toward healthy independence. By Giving Room to Frankie's development and to her relationship with him, Joanne fostered a new, deeper mother-son relationship for years to come.

I hope you'll watch out when someone gives the advice "Go with your gut!" Too often, the guidance our gut gives is like a runaway train, careening downhill with little time or willingness to apply the brakes. Instinctively reacting to our immediate feelings can often lead to regret and frustration. Giving Room to sidestep the feelings in one's gut helps foster understanding in all relationships. Unfortunately, denying your attention to, or delaying expression of, the feelings is not an easy task. When feelings hit, they hit like a ton of bricks! It's hard to calm ourselves when we are flooded with intense emotions. At times, it is helpful to try to set aside the feelings and focus solely on healthy behaviors. In doing so, we are often left pleasantly surprised with a clearer understanding of how to continue to move through life in a healthy manner.

WHO IS IN YOUR CORNER?

Every now and then, Hollywood is not far off in its characterization of shrinks. Like the Robin Williams character in *Good Will Hunting*, I push for my patients to do most of the talking when they come to see me for the first time. (During the initial contact, my staff gathers information about the patient, only a sentence or two, about why he or she is seeking therapy. These responses range from "depressive symptoms" to "I'm getting panic attacks" to "My kid is a hellion," etc.).

After introducing myself, I casually point to their file on my desk and give them my set line: "So, I have read your file, but probably the best way to start off is to tell me what brings you in." After this "what brings you in" statement, the flow of our first gathering is up to the patient. Some like to ramble about their issues. Others are tight-lipped and give one-word answers. There are patients who are very direct about what their goals are in therapy and what they expect from me. And certainly some individuals are vague in their responses.

No matter how the client presents, I have a list of questions in my head that I use to get the person talking. These are questions that you would expect to hear your first time in a shrink's office: How long have the symptoms been present? Tell me about your family. Have you experienced any traumatic events in your life? Tell me about work. Do you have feelings of wanting to hurt yourself? I ask these questions in no specific order. It is the client who is leading our first dance. One of my primary goals during the initial interview is to gather information, but just as important to me is to observe how the person's mind flows. For example: Does the client jump from thought to thought? Are these shifts smooth or abrupt? Does the client reveal true vulnerable emotions or is his or her mind cluttered with defenses? Then, when the client gives me an opening in the rhythmic waltz of our words, I move on to the next question.

But there is one question that I always ask during a first meeting with a client. I make sure of it. If I see that there are only fifteen minutes left in the session and the question has not yet been asked, I just jump in and say, "Sorry to interrupt, but let me ask you this: *Who is in your corner?* You know, who is that person, or even a couple of people, who have always given you that feeling? You know, that *feeling*. That feeling that they are there for you no matter what. That they are in your corner."

The response from this stranger sitting on my couch seeking help is vital information to me in understanding the work that needs to be done in the weeks, months, or even years to come. "Who is in your corner?" If the client is silent and then responds sadly, "There really hasn't been anyone," my heart sinks. I am able to put on a bland poker face when I hear these words, but on the inside I am mourning for this person. Having no one in your corner throughout your entire life is a trauma in and of itself. That might sound melodramatic, but I am telling you, the absence of even one person in your corner, a person who makes you feel supported and cared for, who makes you feel *held*, is, to me, comparable to abuse.

Many developmental theories in psychology have been advanced over the years about the importance of healthy early bonds in a child's life. In essence, these theories stress the vital need to have someone in your corner. And the earlier you had that someone in your corner, the better! Sure, these theorists have argued about what constitutes the "correct" steps or stages of healthy childhood development, and most use different conceptual frameworks to describe their unique take on a child's psychic development. But if I had some of these big-gun psychology gurus sitting on the couch in my office—Sigmund Freud, his daughter Anna, Jean Piaget, Erik Erikson, John Watson, Heinz Kohut, and so on (now that is a funny image!)— I would bet money that all of them would nod their heads in agreement if I asked, "Don't you believe that relationships play a big role in human development?" It's a psychological no-brainer! You don't need to be a famous psychological theorist to realize that having someone in your corner, preferably at an early age in life, is usually essential to a long, happy life.

Social-separation primate studies over the past thirty years have underscored the critical importance of having someone in your corner. Simply stated, during these experiments, some monkeys were separated from their mothers at birth and isolated for several days. I remember cringing in my social psychology class at the pictures of these isolated monkeys, curled up in a ball in the corner of their cages. Their facial expressions communicated pure desolation. Gosh, I get sad just thinking about that image. When these baby monkeys were reunited with their mothers they clung, white-knuckled, to Mom's chest as if they were rock climbing, close to the peak, and wondering why the hell they're hanging in the air at ten thousand feet, one slip away from plunging to their death! While relieved to be holding onto their mothers, these monkeys certainly didn't feel they were out of the danger zone. Extended studies of these deprived monkeys—those without that needed mother in their corner—proved just as grim. As adults, they were often depressed loners and at high risk of neglecting or abusing their own offspring. Those first several days of life alone were costly for these monkeys.

D. W. Winnicott, a pediatrician and psychoanalyst who later became famous for his studies of child development, emphasized the need to have someone in one's corner, even if that person wasn't the perfect caregiver. Dr. Winnicott's concept of *The Good-Enough Mother* was simple. He found that people don't necessarily need the "Super Mom"—the mother with only the most superior qualities and characteristics. According to Dr. Winnicott, we all need affection, love, guidance, consistency, and physical protection, but we don't need to have a perfect or exceptional mom to thrive. Winnicott's theory stresses the need to just be there, physically and psychologically. That is key to having someone in your corner. First and foremost, they have to show up to the dance! By receiving just enough of the good qualities of parenting, kids will do just fine.

Believe it or not, I was actually in psychotherapy myself, years ago, and my experience provides a good example of the importance of having someone in my corner. During my first week of graduate school for my doctoral degree, I received a handwritten note in my school mailbox from Dr. Miller, the department head:

Mr. Castro,

Over the next several years you will experience many learning opportunities while working toward the goal of becoming a clini-

cian. *In our program, the academic studies will be enlightening and the hands-on practicum experience offered through our clinic will help shape your skills as a practicing psychologist. I expect our breadth of training and teaching will serve you well professionally in the years to come.*

My belief when it comes to mental health is that in order to help our patients to the best of our ability, we too need to be patients ourselves. By undergoing your own psychotherapy and experiencing what it is like being on the other side of the couch, you will be able to learn how your own issues impact your work as a psychologist. Rest assured, being in therapy is not a requirement for this program. But if you are interested in beginning psychotherapy, I can be of assistance with several referral names. The entire department is excited to have you join us as you embark on this great endeavor! Welcome!

Dr. James Miller

"Being in therapy is not a requirement . . ." Yeah, right!! The way I read that letter was, "You better get your butt in therapy ASAP or you will amount to nothing in this program!" Nevertheless, Dr. Miller's letter excited me. I knew that every incoming student got some form of "the letter," but the personal tone of Dr. Miller's note made me feel cared for and that he was in my corner. I was still a cocky kid back then, and the thought hadn't crossed my mind that I might actually need therapy. I looked at his offer as a way of joining in on a fun game. As with many situations in my life, I spent little time pondering what I was really getting myself into and impulsively dove in headfirst. (In other words, I listened to my gut and did not delay that gut reaction. I broke all the rules, which, in this case, turned out to be a good thing!)

Dr. Randi Finger lived in a beautiful three-story brownstone in northwest Washington, DC. Like many psychoanalysts, Dr. Finger treated patients out of her home. Her instructions were: "When you first walk in the door from the backyard, you will be in a waiting room with some chairs. Sit down and I will come get you." Immediately to the left of where I waited was a spiral staircase leading up to Dr. Finger's private office. In three years of therapy, I can remember just one time that I saw Dr. Finger walk down those stairs. That was the day we met. Before every session that followed (roughly three per week), she would just open her office door and loudly say hello. That was my cue to walk on up.

After I followed her up those stairs, we headed for the therapy section of her office, which was tucked away in a far corner of the room. Dr. Finger then gave me a choice: sit in a chair or on "The Couch." She seemed to have no preference, so I chose the chair. The couch wouldn't come into play for a few months. I sat back in the chair and smiled. She leaned back in her leather lounge chair, folded her hands, and stared at me. There was no "Welcome, Anthony! Tell me about yourself! I'm glad you're here!" It was just silence for what seemed like eternity.

"Well, I guess I'll just start by talking about myself," I chuckled nervously. And that is how it all began. My therapy experience is another book in itself, but there is a key point I would like to share about my work with Dr. Finger. Through it all, she communicated to me, "I am in your corner. I am here to help, and I care." It wasn't her words that made me feel that I was being supported. Dr. Finger was diligent about holding that blank-slate stance, rarely showing much emotion and speaking very little. I learned from her *words*, but it was her *actions* that made me feel safe and held.

Dr. Finger didn't waver from the routine. Not once. In the waiting room there was a digital clock. My appointment started at 2:30 p.m. Within seconds of the clock ticking from 2:29 to 2:30, her door would burst open and she would summon me. Similarly, when she spoke the words "our time is up for today," I would rise and glance at the clock. It always read 3:15 on the dot. Not 3:14, not 3:16. It was always 3:15. And she always closed our session with those six words: "Our time is up for today." I'd get up while she remained seated. The only time her closing sentence changed was at our last session. Then there were only four words: "Our time is up."

Perhaps you get the sense that Dr. Finger is a cold, unemotional person. When I described to friends how rigid she was with her start and stop times, they would comment, "That doesn't sound very friendly!" I'm sure her style of therapy didn't suit everyone. As a therapist, my own style is very different from that of Dr. Finger. I can be very chatty. I smile a lot, I often nod my head in agreement, and I occasionally run late. But as weird as it may sound, it was Dr. Finger's *consistency* and *predictability* that made me feel secure and cared for. I knew that, come therapy day, her door would always open right at 2:30 p.m. This may sound like a bit of a stretch, but just as when an infant cries and within five seconds Mommy comes running, I felt similar comfort in knowing that Dr. Finger would be there, same time, same day, no matter what.

Only one time in three years did she ever cancel a session. She had left a message the night before, briefly explaining that she was sick. I could barely understand her; she sounded like a dying cow in the middle of a pasture, coughing every few seconds and hardly able to get the words out. I had a big smile on my face as I replayed the message several times. I thought of

113

how angry she must feel not being able to live up to her end of our relationship. Two thirty p.m. would strike tomorrow and no door would open. The situation reminded me of how crushed first-time parents are when they drop the ball and feel that they are not living up to their standards of good parenting. Dr. Finger's reliable and inevitable way of relating to me fostered my ability to trust. Sure, she was the doctor and I was the patient, but her caring stance made me feel like we were a "We," teammates passionately focused on working together trusting each other to accomplish our common goal.

My guess, at this point, is that you get it. You understand that the ongoing presence throughout your life of someone in your corner, someone who has *held you*—figuratively if not literally, is critical to living a contented life. You buy my idea that a child with no one in his corner suffers just as if he were being emotionally abused. You feel for the lonely monkeys separated from their mothers, just as I do, and understand that these little primates are in for a difficult life. And you grasp the theory of the good-enough mother. It is not perfection; it is a psychological and physical presence that is vital, just as with Dr. Finger. Now you may be saying, "I never had that good-enough mother; I never had that person in my corner. What do I do?"

If no one is, or ever has been, in your corner, it is time to Give Room and allow it. If you were deprived of it as a child, my guess is that letting a person into your life to play the role of "being in your corner" is extremely difficult for you. Life is about relationships and humility. Your willingness to lean on others is required in order to Give Room. Also consider the give-take, or narcissist-masochist continuum. Are you Giving Room to let more people in your corner? Or can you Give Room to let people who are already in your corner (even though you may not be aware that they *are* in your corner) further in, at a deeper level? Giving Room to relationships, to having someone in your corner, is what we humans were meant to do. Most of us have the skill to maneuver our way through life alone. But let's face it—life is so much more enjoyable when you have someone on your side and in your corner, sharing this magnificent experience called life.

Chapter Three

GIVING ROOM FOR OTHERS TO GROW

When we adults think of children there is a simple truth which we ignore: childhood is not preparation for life; childhood is life. A child isn't getting ready to live, a child is living.

Children are constantly confronted with the nagging question: "What are you going to be?" Courageous would be the youngster who, looking the adult squarely in the face, would say, "I'm not going to be anything; I already am." We adults would be shocked by such an insolent remark, for we have forgotten, if indeed we ever knew, that a child is an active, participating and contributing member of society from the time of birth. Childhood isn't a time when a pre-human is molded into a human who will then live life; the child is a human who is living life. No child will miss the zest and joy of living unless these are denied him by adults who have convinced themselves that childhood is a period of preparation.

How much heartache we would save ourselves if we would recognize children as partners with adults in the process of living, rather than always viewing them as apprentices. How much we could teach each other; we have the experience and they have the freshness. How full both our lives could be.

The children may not lead us, but at least we ought to discuss the trip with them, for, after all, life is their journey, too.

—John H. Taylor, *Notes on an Unhurried Journey*

KIDS ARE PEOPLE, TOO!

Over the summer, all the ministers at my church go somewhere. I don't know exactly what they do or where they go . . . climb to the top of a mountain for forty days and nights, hang out at Club Med, who knows. So it is up to the members of the church to lead and prepare a service every Sunday during the summer months. Eliot Chapel is a Unitarian Universalist church. I love our church because it is accepting of all individuals and all spiritual beliefs. My church loves everyone! Christmas and Hanukkah are celebrated. There is even a service once a year to "bless your pets"! Now that is fun, watching all those dogs parade down the center aisle of the chapel as the entire congregation sings praises to their four-legged family members. At Eliot, you can say virtually anything you want and the congregation will nod and smile and accept you with open arms. When my friends ask, "So what do Unitarians believe in?" they struggle with my formal answer: "Our church's mission is to foster free religious

thought, nurture spiritual growth, and act for social justice."
My informal answer clears things up. "The Unitarian Universalist Church is kind of like Switzerland, staying in the neutral
zone and allowing consideration of all possibilities."

Soon after my wife and I joined the church, we had the
opportunity to lead one of these services. Together we chose
the music and the readings, and eventually I prepared and
delivered the sermon. The topic I chose was "gender issues."
That Sunday morning in August, feeling a little nervous yet
very excited, I spoke about how little boys and little girls are
raised differently in Western society and how our actions with
our kids impact their relationships with others throughout life.
When I finished the sermon I sat back in my pew and basked
in the warm reception. "Wow, I really helped to educate my
fellow congregants! They must love me!"

As it turns out, however, while I was patting myself on the
back, the congregation was on its feet for someone else! It
wasn't *my* sermon that got the attention of my fellow church
members. After my sermon, my wife had taken the pulpit and
read the above quotation as the final reading. I have always
loved that quote, but let's be honest, *my* sermon was prepared
by a doctor of psychology and was therefore much deeper than
the simple message "childhood is not just a time of preparation for adulthood." That Sunday morning, my sermon, lov-
ingly woven with some pretty good psychobabble, did get positive feedback, but it was my wife's reading that really got
everyone excited. Many people came up to Missy and me after
the service to say what a great message that reading delivered
and how it got them thinking about the central point: kids are
living; they are not just preparing to live.

It is a strong message that speaks to a culture caught up in the all-consuming Rat Race. Many of the psychological theories advanced over the years about child development are based on *stages*. As with my "to-do list," on Saturday mornings (mow the lawn, fix the front door, take daughter to T-ball, etc.), each successive developmental stage gets checked off. Some of the greatest master theorists—Freud, Erikson, Kernberg, Piaget— have emphasized the stages of child development. I believe the sentiments expressed in the above quotation guide us away from the "stages model" and nudge us toward a more fluid mode of living in the present with our children.

As I describe my father, please understand two things. Number one, I love my dad. And number two, his behavior when it comes to his children is definitely not normal (which might explain my career path!). During my childhood, my father fell into this trap of seeing his kids as always transitioning rather than simply living. Dad was a firm believer in society's powerful assumption that children are working toward "an end" and that childhood is just a necessary evil you must endure until life *really* begins.

There's a well-known saying that "childhood is an illness that fortunately can be cured." Sometimes I think this quote could be attributed to my dad! "Illness" may be a bit over the top, but my father's "keep pushing and don't look back" attitude hindered us kids from Giving Room to appreciate and enjoy our accomplishments. For example, when my brother Paul earned his brown belt in karate, my dad's response was not congratulatory but rather one of prodding inquiry. "So, Paul, now what are your plans for getting your black belt?" When my sister Mary Jo happily spent hours creating beautiful paintings, my father was busy researching the best art schools for ten-year-olds. My older brother Stephen's acceptance into the Naval Academy was no occasion to celebrate, according to Dad. On the contrary, all my dad had to say was, "Now it is time to prepare for your first week at the Academy. Everyone will be trying to take you down!" My brother Dave might have been the most fortunate son. He actually received a quick pat on the back when, at the young age of nineteen, he became head manager at the largest movie theater in town. But it wasn't long before Dad began focusing on developing a strategy for Dave to become the youngest regional manager in the movie chain! For Dad, there was no time to embrace these childhood successes. His view was that you must always keep pushing forward or everything might slip away.

Dad's steady refrain was "Plan and think big!" He always managed to slip in a few inspirational quotations during our discussions: "Shoot for the moon, and if you miss, you will still be among the stars!" His favorite was, "Losers let it happen; winners *make* it happen!"

This message clearly motivates one to take charge and make something of his or her life. Yet I also believe that this attitude is at odds with the idea (expressed in the quotation above) that it is okay for children, in particular, to let things play out more organically. Constant striving and planning pushes us away from being "in the moment" and embracing life around us.

Being the son of immigrants and living in poverty, my father felt like a survivor as a kid. It makes sense that he honed in on accomplishing goals and moving forward. It also explains why he pushed my siblings and me to (here comes another of Dad's infamous quotes) "Be the best! Be Number 1!" But I believe, at times, that being Number 2 or 7 is okay and much more realistic. As I discussed earlier, this points to

121

the fact that life is a continuum of possibilities. Funny thing is, by embracing the reality that you will not always be Number 1, you actually Give Yourself Room and free up energy to work toward reaching your potential. Surprisingly, by Giving Room and accepting that you may be Number 2, you may find that you end up being Number 1 more often!

Recently a parent said to me, with pride, "I tell my kids we're an 'A family.' There is no room for B's, let alone C's in our family!" That statement sent shivers down my spine! I said to the mom, "Do you mean to tell me you don't allow any room for your family to just be average?" We went on to discuss the pressure her kids must feel to "be the best" and how this has led them to look at life as a checklist, with the last item reading, "Childhood: complete." Time to check it off!

How enriching life would be if we parents embraced our kids as complete people with a lot to offer *right now, today!* This is not to say that having goals is a bad thing. In fact, much like my father, I, too, am competitive and goal-oriented (and also a sucker for inspirational quotes!). There is nothing that gets my adrenaline flowing more than an intense game of Ping-Pong or billiards—or a book of famous inspirational quotes! But too often, our goals, when combined with the pressures of society, are interpreted as "Forward march!" rather than "Embrace the moment!" We would serve our children well to let them know it's okay to Give Room and to experience life. Meet with your children and encourage them to live and express themselves *now*, at this very moment. You may be surprised at the dreams your children reveal if you simply Give Them Room.

MEN'S ISSUES?

On the first day of my predoctoral internship I was required to attend a one-on-one meeting with John Yurich, the director of training. John was a very handsome man in his early forties. His goatee was slightly sprinkled with gray and his hair was long, brown, and wavy. A reality TV makeover could have instantly turn John into a movie star—he was that striking. John talked very softy and always looked you in the eye when he spoke. A "gentle man" is how most people would describe him, yet for all his ease, John's words were quite assertive. A seasoned psychologist, John was nationally known as an excellent clinician and trainer. His unique specialty in the field was "men's issues."

On the day of our meeting, I thought, *men's issues, what does that mean?* Sure, I knew about well-known men's books like *Iron John*. And I had read about those "men's therapeutic weekends," where a bunch of men, beating on drums and running around, meet out in the wilderness with war paint smeared all over their faces. These gatherings are meant to reconnect men with their manhood and help them bond as brothers.

As it turned out, John Yurich was pretty normal. As our meeting began I quickly felt at ease talking to John. I felt secure and comfortable in his presence. John described what the year would entail and the various duties for which I would be responsible. Our dialogue was rhythmic, like two friends leisurely volleying a tennis ball back and forth. Then came *the* question.

John asked, "Anthony, what types of clients do you like to work with?"

I thought, *Is this a trick question?* I responded hesitantly,

"Well, John, as you know, I have worked with kids and adolescents, and I have experience with adults. Oh, and obviously I really enjoy college students; that's why I'm so happy to be here at the Student Counseling Center."

John smiled. "I'm sorry, Anthony. Let me be clearer. Do you prefer working with male or female clients?"

I didn't know what to say. I had never even thought about it. For a good thirty seconds, I didn't say anything, and John just sat there, patiently waiting for my answer. Yet, the more I thought about his question, the more I realized the answer was obvious. I explained to John that I felt more helpful as a therapist for my female clients than for the males. The therapeutic bond was much stronger and more quickly established with women. I was able to empathize more freely about their issues. And the dropout rate for women was drastically lower. As I was rambling on about all the great work I had done with women in therapy settings and the frequent failures with my male clients, I started to freak out. What a discrepancy! The flaw was suddenly as apparent and painful as a freshly skinned knee.

John softly asked, "Now, why is that the case, Anthony? Why do you struggle when working with men?"

I remarked honestly, "I don't know."

John gave me a reassuring smile. "Well, I think that would be a great focus to have this year . . . to find out why."

John and I talked about my uncomfortable feelings around male patients and how I communicated little empathy or interest. This led to many edifying discussions about *gender role conflict*. John stressed how, especially in Western culture, boys are raised (at times to an extreme) to be independent, competitive, and unemotional. The message to boys is "Win at all costs, never show your cards, and claw your way to the top of the heap!" (Sound familiar?) Conversely, girls are raised to be relational. It is *okay* to express emotions if you are a girl. Girls are encouraged and praised when they join with others in intimate communication. For example, it is no surprise that my three-year-old daughter Zinnia is constantly begging me to play dolls. Our play is filled with feelings and interactions. We change the dolls' diapers; we feed the dolls. The dolls talk to each other and let the other dolls know if they are feeling sick or happy or sad. We communicate, we play, and we create dialogue. Zinnia enjoys the play and she is praised for it.

John's message was simple. Gender role conflict occurs when boys and men adhere *too rigidly* to society's male gender roles. In my research, I learned about the high risk of depression and alcoholism in men struggling with this conflict. Little boys who were pushed to be extremely independent and competitive tended to have a difficult time balancing family life and work. Also, many men had limited ability to express emotions, leading to discord and misunderstanding when trying to form meaningful relationships. I read about men hyperfocused on accumulating money, power, and sex partners. So many of them end up feeling alone, hopeless, and angry at the world.

The more I learned from John and the more I reviewed the various research materials, the more times I said to myself, "Well, well! So this is what Dr. Finger's therapy sessions were all about!" Was I among the more extreme sufferers of gender role conflict? I didn't think so. But certainly my upbringing had engrained in me the will to "be the best; win at all costs" and above all to "be number one!" My dad would at times even embellish the "be number one" message by proclaiming, "Be number one, because number two is right behind you, ready to screw you over!" Now that's not just being competitive, that's survival! As I became more and more familiar with gender role conflict, I thought, "Hmm, some of this stuff sounds real familiar."

A few months into my internship year, Missy and I flew back to DC to celebrate Thanksgiving with my family. I was excited to get a break from all this gender role conflict stuff. Unfortunately, I was about to see this conflict come to life right before my eyes. It occurred as I was driving from break-fast with my elder brother, Frank and his family. Frank and his wife, Kathleen, were in the front seat, and I was in the back with their nine-year-old son, Jason, and their seven-year-old daughter, Ann. Jason was upset that he was not allowed to go over to a friend's house to play. He pleaded with his parents as tears filled his eyes and his voice quivered. "There will be two hours before we all have to go to Grandfather and Nonny's house for Thanksgiving. Can't I just go over to Brendan's house for a little bit?"

For a while, my brother ignored his son's whining. But then he exploded, "No, Jason! You are not going to Brendan's house, and for God's sake, stop crying like a girl!"

At that moment everything around me slowed down in a surreal way, and I started to feel nauseated. I remember feeling like an outsider looking in. I couldn't believe what I had just heard: *stop crying like a girl.* Interestingly, my brother and his wife immediately went back into their conversation with little emotion, as if nothing had happened. I looked at Jason. He hung his head, sniffling as he tried desperately to stop crying. He raked at his eyes, wiping the tears away.

I glanced at Ann. She looked both sad and confused. I imagined her thinking, *Sometimes I cry—is that bad? I'm a girl—is that bad?*

As my mentor, John, said, "These powerful messages from society are all around us; open your ears to hear them. If you don't hear them, you can't change things." In so many ways, my brother and sister-in-law are model parents. Frank is a dedicated father who spends much of his time coaching his kids' sports teams or just lying on the floor on a lazy Sunday afternoon doing a puzzle with Jason and Ann. He is a proactive dad who cares deeply for his children. And my sister-in-law is a grade-school teacher. She absolutely loves kids and constantly receives praise for teaching youngsters not only their ABC's but also what it means to be a humble and kind human being. Yet this example illustrates how even model parents can sow the seeds of gender conflict at an early age, potentially causing future problems.

We've all made comments that reinforce the message that *for males to express strong feelings is weak, feminine, and wrong.* In the memorable words of Arnold Schwarzenegger, one must avoid being a "girlie-man" at all costs! Like my brother, many of us don't realize that a simple comment such as "Stop crying like a girl" can have negative consequences on the development of our kids. Such a comment communicates, "Don't feel! Don't show emotions! Showing feelings is weak!" How often have you observed in an emotionally charged situation, like a funeral, the birth of a child, or a wedding ceremony, the men in these situations freely shedding tears? Unfortunately, very seldom, if at all.

I learned during that training year in Seattle that men *do* feel, but it is very hard for them to express and really understand those feelings. It was certainly a struggle for me, being raised in a home that stressed winning rather than expressing emotions. This dynamic is everywhere. Take, for example, a male athlete being interviewed after the big game and shunning the camera as tears fill his eyes. The intense emotions, whether he's won or lost, overwhelm him, and as he begins to cry it "just doesn't feel right." So often, the first words out of his mouth once he collects himself are "I'm sorry." What he's really saying is, "I am sorry for expressing my true feelings. It feels wrong to feel something. By crying, I am doing something foolish, ridiculous, inappropriate, embarrassing, weak, and wrong."

Several times, over the years, a male patient has come into my office and said something like, "My father just passed away. The service was tough but I got through it and stayed strong." I asked, "Did you cry?" Immediately, my patient became uncomfortable, evidently feeling that I was attacking his manhood with what he perceived as a sarcastic question. Defensively, yet also nervously, the bereaved would say, "Well, no, I didn't cry! I just told you, I stayed strong! My dad, God rest his soul, would have been proud!"

Recently, Ed, a sixty-two-year-old, bald, fairly overweight man, suffering from a severe bout of clinical depression, came to see me. He explained that he had been working in a middle school for thirty-plus years as a custodian. For all that time, Ed went about his work like a compliant soldier, serving his duty with a smile on his face. Unfortunately, over the past several months, Ed's depressive symptoms had increased, adversely affecting his work performance. He began calling in sick. His motivation had dropped off drastically, and feelings of hopelessness filled his mind. The school board members knew they couldn't continue to keep Ed on the job, but he was only two years away from retirement and a nice pension plan. Ed kept pushing. He would plead to the board, "I can do it. Things are going to get better. I'll make a turnaround—you'll see." But Ed's depression lingered, and he continually dropped the ball on work tasks. Fortunately, the board didn't fire him. Instead Ed was granted a special exemption of an early retirement with full pension benefits.

As Ed explained his story, his eyes would water up every few minutes. Valiantly fighting the tears, he'd say, "Just give me a second . . . I'm okay." Then he would go on.

After about thirty minutes of Ed fighting his intense emotions but really wanting and clearly needing to cry, I stopped him. I asked, "Ed, why do you keep stopping yourself from crying?"

He stuttered, "Well, I don't want to . . . uhhh . . . you know, uh, I want to hold it together."

I said, "Ed, do you realize how refreshing it is for me to meet a grown man who can actually cry so easily? I know you're depressed, but still I am in awe of you that you can let out such intense feelings so easily. It's such a gift you have."

You would have thought a thousand-pound weight was lifted off his shoulders. Ed's body loosened, he sank back into the couch, and nodded with a smile as tears filled his eyes. He was so relieved and happy to hear that I was not only nonjudgmental about his tears but that I actually admired him for his *ability* to express his feelings. The more Ed Gave Room to let it all out in therapy, the more his depression lifted.

I get so excited and shake my head in envy when I come across men who can let their feelings flow freely. In my experience, both professionally and personally, it's a very rare occurrence. Matt Woolley, my longtime friend from college, has the ability to open up like this. Matt has no problem crying in front of us old college buddies. The tears are likely to start flowing whether he has won our annual golf tournament or we're listening to the eulogy at our friend's father's funeral. Matt lives on the East Coast, and whenever I know I'm going to see him I'm filled with delightful anticipation. When we embrace after not seeing each other for many months, his eyes are always watery with happiness. His *gift* helps my eyes water, too.

Another occasion that brought tears to my eyes was several years ago at the renowned professional golf tournament, the Masters. The tournament came down to a two-man race between Len Matice and Mike Weir. Mike Weir eventually won the tournament in a sudden-death playoff, but it was Len Matice's incredible final round, shooting in the low sixties on Championship Sunday, that got him in the playoff in the first place.

After the tournament, Len was interviewed by a swarm of reporters. As question after question was fired his way, Len answered with tears streaming down his face. He didn't shy away from the cameras. He didn't pause to "gather himself," "compose himself," "get a hold of himself," or "pull himself together." He simply answered the questions and cried. It was obvious that some of the reporters (predominantly men) were starting to feel uncomfortable with Len's free expression of emotions. One of these reporters asked in a tentative voice, "You seem really shaken, Len. What is going on inside of you?"

Still weeping, Len smiled and, in so many words, he responded, "I'm proud of myself. I played well and I'm happy. I'm obviously disappointed that I lost in the end. But the point is, I have a lot of intense emotions right now and that's good."

☼ ☼ ☼

As my predoctoral internship training year was coming to a close, I was feeling overwhelmed. Missy and I were expecting our first child in a few months and we'd made the decision to relocate to St. Louis and start our family. I had applied for several jobs in the St. Louis area and had been on a few interviews, but no employment opportunities had developed. I sullenly said to John, "I just don't understand it. I thought I would have a job secured by now. I only have three weeks left before I move."

I waited for him to begin strategizing with me about jobs. Maybe he would tweak my resume? Or possibly we would do some mock interviews together? He had already written some great recommendation letters for me, but, I thought, maybe he was also willing to make a few phone calls on my behalf. Instead, John said, "Anthony, you haven't found a job yet. There is a very good chance that if you keep pursuing opportunities over the next couple of months in St. Louis, you will be offered a job as a psychologist. I can almost guarantee it. But if I were you, I might reconsider that approach.

"As I understand it, Missy is going to work until the baby arrives and then just work part-time, at the most. I was just thinking, why not switch it around? Sounds to me like you may have a nice opportunity to devote the next couple of years to raising your daughter."

It all made sense. All the teaching, learning, and supervision that I had experienced that year in Seattle suddenly came together for me. His advice reopened my eyes and Gave Room to the reality that I had *choices* and that I didn't need to be captive to the rigid societal stereotypes that had been inculcated in me. These are the very stereotypes that hinder men from Giving Room and seeing all the possibilities in life. It hadn't even crossed my mind that I had the unbelievable option to be a stay-at-home dad! I was so caught up in "achieving the next task on the list" that I had forgotten just about everything I had learned about that formerly elusive term, *men's issues*. John was right. A great opportunity was staring me in the face, one that most men rarely get, and I hadn't Created Space in my mind to see it! What a gift it would be to my daughter and to myself to Give Room to be her primary caregiver! What an experience it would be for me to embrace such an awesome job!

John smiled. "It's probably the best job offer you'll ever get, and you don't even have to interview for it!"

THE URGENCY TO GIVE

As most of us know, Dr. Martin Luther King Jr.'s most famous words were "I have a dream!" That passionate speech he delivered in our nation's capital has gone down in history as a turning point in human rights. Thankfully, over the past forty years, we have witnessed Dr. King's dream becoming more and more of a reality every day. But let me share another of Dr. King's quotes that I find just as powerful (remember, I am a sucker for inspirational quotes!). Dr. King said, "Life's most persistent and urgent question is: What are you doing for others?"

The word that sticks out in my mind when reflecting on this quote is *urgent*. Most of us feel that it is nice to help others. Giving a little can go a long way. It doesn't take much to help the little old lady struggling to cross the road or to wave the person in line behind you to step ahead at the grocery checkout. But Dr. King feels that giving is an *urgent* issue. When the time is right or it is convenient, most of us have good intentions, but when helping becomes inconvenient, we often turn our backs or make excuses. In other words, giving is not a priority.

Dr. King's words convey the obvious truth that helping others benefits the recipient. But to me, the magic in his statement is the unspoken suggestion that in feeling and honoring an imperative to help, both the giver and the receiver win! We all know how good it feels to help. The more that we adults communicate to our youth the importance and thrill of giving, the more space is created for happiness in their lives.

We all know giving is a good thing. The way it relates to Giving Room is that the act of giving Creates Space for both the giver and the receiver to slow down in life and appreciate what is really important; it allows them time to reflect. Giving Room to tend to each other's needs is a gateway to personal fulfillment.

During the holiday season, I usually ask my young patients, "So, what's on your Hanukkah or Christmas list this year?" Without fail, almost all of these kids respond with exuberance as they rattle off the Game Boys, Yu-Gi-Oh! cards, iPods, and so on that they are hoping to receive. But an interesting thing happens when I ask, "Tell me about the gifts you're planning to *give*." The kids who are self-centered and have low self-esteem offer brief responses, with little emotion. However, the kids who possess a strong sense of self, healthy self-esteem, and genuine humility tend to elaborate in great detail about their plans to give. And their descriptions of giving burst with emotion! To them, the giving side of the holiday season is just as gratifying as the receiving. So what do my observations tell me? Simply that kids who are *encouraged* to give are mentally healthier than kids whose parents do not stress the importance—and the delight—of giving.

A nice way to incorporate this value as a parent is through an allowance. I am a big believer in giving kids an allowance for the completion of their family responsibilities and chores, such as feeding the dog or taking out the trash. Giving an allowance is great on many levels. First, next time you are in Target with little Jacob and he starts screaming, "Mommy, I want this toy!" all you have to say is, "Sounds good, Jacob, but did you bring your money?" This will often stop kids in their tracks. The child may be flooded with frustration when you communicate, "If you want it, buy it yourself," but exposing kids to frustration is a good thing. (Later I will get more into building frustration tolerance in kids, as well as teaching them the importance of money.)

Besides helping you get out of the "I want! I want! I want!" dance with your kids, an allowance is a great tool for teaching the importance of giving. You say to your child, "Okay, Jake. You did a great job with your family chores this week. That means you earned your four-dollar allowance." At this point, it is vitally important to actually hand your child the four bucks (or four quarters, or four dimes—whatever amount you feel comfortable with). Then you continue, "Now, Jake, two of those dollars are for you to do whatever you want with." Jake pulls out the wallet he got for his birthday from Grandma and shoves two of the four bucks in. You continue. "One of the remaining dollars goes into your bank account for you to save." At this point, Jake hands back one of the dollars and nods, agreeing that you will put the dollar into the savings account that you opened up together. Then you add, "And the final dollar is the *Giving Dollar*. Let's talk about how you might want to give your dollar away to someone who really needs it."

You are not encouraging your little boy to donate one of his dollars. You are *requiring* it. However, he does have the freedom to give the dollar to whatever person or organization he chooses. Just as important as making giving a requirement, granting Jake the freedom to actively think about where he wants his dollar to go is key in assisting him to develop the independence and leadership to help others in life. Jake's parents are pushing their son into an unknown space. It is this space that creates happiness and Gives Room for change. The child has the choice as to where the money goes, but you, the parent, certainly may assist in helping him to think through his decision. This can be a great moment of bonding between parent and child, as they brainstorm about where the dollar should go. Jake says, "Mommy, I was thinking that if I save my Giving Dollar for ten weeks I would have ten Giving Dollars, and then I could give the ten dollars to the nice man ringing that bell with the red jar outside the grocery store." Or he says, "Daddy, let's go drive to the nursing home where Great-Grandpa used to live and give my dollar to them. I'm sure they need it."

As a parent, you need to react to your child's ideas about giving just as seriously and with the same enthusiasm as he does. You jump up with excitement! "Great idea, Jake! Let's look at the calendar and pick the exact date when we will visit the man with the red jar." "Excellent choice, Jake! Let's call Carol, the director of the nursing home, and let her know we are on our way!"

Another example of teaching kids the importance and the joy of giving is by requiring them to do a summer project. This could be donating time to volunteer at a nonprofit organization, delivering food to a food bank, taking a neighbor's dog for a daily walk, and so on. The more active and involved the child is, the better. If you can tailor the project to the child's talents, all the better. For example, Zoe is a great artist and loves animals. This past summer, Zoe's project was simple. She drew a cute picture of herself walking our dog. Then, with the assistance of her mother, she had greeting cards created with the picture on the front.

The cost was roughly fifty cents to make each card. My wife and I donated to Zoe's project by providing her the twenty-five dollars to get the initial fifty cards printed. Then Zoe was off! Knocking on neighbors' doors, she explained that she was selling the cards to raise money for Stray Rescue of St. Louis, a nonprofit organization that takes in and finds good homes for dogs that have been abandoned. We were hoping that she'd be able to sell all fifty cards by the end of the summer. Yet, once again, we learned how giving is contagious when one makes it a priority. Zoe sold her fifty cards by the end of the first *week*! By the end of the summer, she had sold more cards than any of us imagined possible. Everyone loved the cards and demanded more. It was a thrilling moment for our little girl, beaming with happiness and confidence, to present over one hundred dollars to the director of Stray Rescue. Zoe's project Created Space and Gave Room for her to experience that special moment, which allowed her character and confidence to grow.

When we focus on giving to others, our personal problems don't seem so big. Several days after the 9/11 attacks, I was talking with my brother about the horrible event. As we were talking, he remarked, "Hey, buddy, since you're a psychologist, I got a great question for you. Every day at the center we get hundreds of calls [my brother volunteers at the suicide prevention center in Los Angeles]. We have over half a dozen counselors taking call after call, 24/7. So why was it that on the day of the attacks we received zero calls? All day we were sitting around and the phones were silent."

I didn't have an answer for him then, but I do now, and I think the answer is directly related to the idea of giving. Everyone in the country was glued to their TV sets on 9/11. The country was in shock as our hearts mourned for the victims and their families. All of our energy and emotions were being *given* to others. All those depressed and traumatized Californians who would normally be calling the hotline center were like the rest of us. Their thoughts were not on themselves. For one day, we all did something healthy: We stopped thinking about ourselves and gave our hearts and resources to those in need. Everywhere you turned, people were proactively supporting others. People focused on giving. Millions of dollars were donated by the hour. American flags were quickly sold out. Marches of support occurred all over the country. By uniting as one in such a giving way, there was no time to be depressed. Our focus was on helping, and although we were frightened and in mourning, there was a positive energy that filled us all.

To me, this much is clear: The act of giving simply makes one feel better. Whether it is through the Giving Dollar, a summer project, or just holding the door open for a stranger, when we give, we grow. And when we grow, we are Giving Room. Doing for others should not just be an act of convenience; giving to others should be an *urgent* and not always comfortable priority. When one thoughtfully and deliberately Gives Room to give—when we instill giving as a priority in our children—everyone benefits.

PARENTING CLASS 101: KIDS AND MONEY

My daughters and I have a ritual every Saturday morning. At 6:00 a.m., I burst into the TV room where they are watching

The Parent Trap for the 252nd time, and I announce, "It's time to hit Schnucks! Let's go!" I pack them into the minivan, and we head off to the grocery store for bacon, eggs, and the all-important cup of java. Before we leave, I make a point to remind Zoe, "You might want to bring your money." Zoe carefully pockets roughly eight bucks that she got from her wallet hidden under her bed.

We buy all the necessities—including that cup of coffee for Dad—and then we hit the last aisle. This is the highlight of the trip—the aisle with the coloring book section. There is quite an extensive selection of coloring books, and I'm prepared to wait in this aisle for at least ten minutes. Zoe begins her search, rubbing her hands and clapping twice. She is excited but also nervous. She glances at me. "So how much is this SpongeBob one?"

I snag the coloring book. "Look here, Zoe. On the back it says $3.99, so it will cost you a little over four bucks, with tax."

Zoe reaches into her pockets and recounts her eight dollars. Hesitantly, she says, "Ah, okay. Let's see what else they got."

The pattern continues: she finds a coloring book, determines the cost, and rechecks the amount of cash in her pocket, weighing the possibilities. When this routine began a few years ago, it was so painful to watch. The agony on Zoe's face of not knowing what to do—*Should I spend the money now* (instant gratification) *or save it for something bigger and better in the future* (delayed gratification)? She used to try to push me to make the decision for her. "What would you do, Daddy?"

I would never tell her what to do. Instead, I'd describe in detail the advantages and disadvantages of buying and saving. My answer often frustrated Zoe and made her anxiety worse. Eventually, she would make a decision. Sometimes she would buy and sometimes she would save.

Finding opportunities to teach kids about money is essential when Giving Room to kids to allow them to grow and mature. Unfortunately, much of our world revolves around money. Money is all around us, woven into the fabric of most everything we do. As adults, we are constantly reminded of the prominent place money has in our lives. This can lead to anger and the overwhelming feeling that "we never have enough." Because of the bitterness or other negative feelings that so many of us have toward money, we frequently shelter our kids from the stresses of this subject. But exposing them to how money impacts emotions is a gift of giving.

I often observe a link between money and emotions when working with teenage patients and their parents. Take, for example, my patient Steven. On his fifteenth birthday, Steven is first in line at the Motor Vehicle Administration (MVA), where he is fully prepared to pass the written learner's permit test. As predicted, he passes with ease. He confidently pumps his fist as he and his mom exit the building, "Yes! Only three hundred and sixty-five days until I'll be driving on my own. Mom, I really love those new Mustangs; do you think we could stop by the Ford dealership and take a look at them?"

Mom becomes nervous and quickly comes up with an excuse. "I've got to get to work, Steven. Maybe some other time." Mom's tension is based on Steven's expectation that he will be given a new car when he turns sixteen. This is not such a lofty expectation on Steven's part, considering that his parents have always told him, "Pass your classes at school and you get a car." Plus, this is the norm in Steven's community: most sixteen-year-olds are given their own set of wheels. But lately, Steven's parents have begun to question the idea of just handing their son a new car. Their doubts aren't based on lack of money but on the fact that over the years they have observed nephews, nieces, and friends' kids being handed the keys to a new car, only to fail to show the maturity to handle such an enormous gift. Frequently, these kids run up speeding tickets, get into several fender benders within months of taking the wheel, and overall neglect their cars by not tending to regularly scheduled maintenance.

I couldn't have agreed more with Steven's parents. In my practice, I witness over and over parents who don't require any contribution from their kids for large gifts, such as a car. Consequently, these kids don't respect and honor the privilege of driving, nor do they see the connection between having something big, like a car, and money. Emotionally, they can't internalize all the financial and tactical dealings that come into play. We all recognize the importance of teaching our children the value of a dollar, however, did you know that turning a gift, such as driving and owning a car, into a lesson in financial awareness for teenagers actually Gives Room? Yes, it Gives Room for emotional growth.

When Steven and his parents first came to see me, they immediately explained their dilemma. "We know Steven is a good kid," the parents said as they tensely glanced over at their son, "but he will be sixteen in less than a year and he's expecting us to just give him a car."

Steven jumped in. "All my friends who are sixteen have cars!"

Steven's father waved his hand. "Son, we want you to drive. Trust me, it would help us out a lot not having to drive you all over the place."

I turned to Steven. "Okay, your parents don't want to just buy you a car. I agree with them. Giving a sixteen-year-old kid a new car just because he turned sixteen and got his license is wrong. Expecting such a large gift is even worse." Steven snarled, but I continued, "Let me finish. Having said that, it sounds like your parents are willing to help out with the cost of a car, which I find is quite a vote of confidence in you and very generous. So, Steven, my question to you is, what do you propose to your parents?"

Like all the fifteen-year-olds to whom I ask this question, Steven responds, "I really don't know what you're talking about."

I don't make it a long, drawn-out disquisition, but I do take a few minutes to explain to Steven that "the grown-up world runs on contracts." Everywhere you look, there is a contract. I explain, "Steven, even for the Blockbuster movie you rented last Friday night, there was a contract involved in that transaction. You know the light switch you turned on when you walked into your room last night in order to see where your DVD player was so that you could insert the movie? Well, there is an 'electricity contract' in place that allows you to see the light! Your parents have a contract with a bank requiring them to pay for your house. So, let's come up with a contract so that you can get that car in three hundred and fifty-five days."

Kids love contracts. Parents are often surprised about how excited kids become when asked to come up with a contract in order to achieve a goal. Parents underestimate their child's feelings when they assume that they would never go for something written out that clearly states, "You do this, and I will do that." I also believe that parents unconsciously fear that if they "spell things out," their child will actually accomplish the goal and then they'll be held accountable for living up to their end of the contract!

Steven's case was a great example of how implementing a contract can fill a teenager's soul with enthusiasm and self-belief. Over the next three sessions, Steven and his parents (with a little help from me, moving the negotiations along by playing the role of the old game-show host Monty Hall of *Let's Make a Deal*) hammered out a contract. Steven's parents felt strongly that their son's primary "job" was to get good grades. So I encouraged them to put a price on report card grades. An A = $400, a B = $200, a C = $0; anything below a C would cost Steven $50 out of the "Car Fund." Steven did the calculations and realized that even if his grades were stellar over the next eleven months, there would only be roughly four grand in the Car Fund by his sixteenth birthday. Certainly enough money to buy a decent used car, but Steven wanted more and was willing to work for it. His parents allowed him to get a part-time job over the weekends and holidays, as long as he worked no more than fifteen hours per week. Mom and Dad were adamant about schoolwork and grades remaining Steven's top priority. Item 2 on the contract read: *For every dollar Steven contributes to the Car Fund, parents will match that dollar.*

Within days, Steven landed a job at the local carwash. "Three great things about this job," he remarked with a smile. "First, it's really good money once you add in tips. Second, I can study during down times while I'm still getting paid, and third, once I get my car, free carwashes, baby!" It was so rewarding for me as a therapist to see Steven excited and focused on a goal. He was empowered by the contract because he had control over it. He owned it! His parents were shocked. Their bratty, underachieving kid, who had always fought against doing homework and chores, was now talking like a confident and responsible young man!

The final details of the contract spelled out that Steven would be responsible for gas, maintenance of the car, and half of the car insurance premiums (insurance would be cheaper for Steven if he maintained at least a 3.0 GPA—yet another incentive for him to make his grades a priority). On his sixteenth birthday, Steven and his parents were once again first in line at the MVA. They were nervous, yet excited. It had turned out to be the most exciting day of the year for all three. Steven's parents allowed their son to skip school, and Steven's dad took the day off. Their son had worked his tail off all year in preparation for this day, and they couldn't have been prouder.

As he exited the testing center with a radiant smile, Steven gave his dad a bear hug. "I told you I'd ace it! No way that I wouldn't pass that test! Look at my picture." Throughout the rest of the day, Steven test-drove used Mustangs at five different dealerships. His Car Fund account had reached $8,723.55— not enough for a new Mustang but certainly enough for a nice used one. As Steven was showing me the pictures of *his* new car I asked, "Are you disappointed you didn't reach a little bit further and earn a little bit more so that you could have gotten a new Mustang?" "No," he said. "I'm going to enjoy this one. But mark my words, Dr. C. By my eighteenth birthday, I will be upgrading to not just a new Mustang but the new turbo convertible Mustang." And yes, Steven did earn that new turbo convertible two years later. Just one problem: I was a little jealous! Scowling as I took in the picture Steven sent me of his beautiful car, I couldn't help but think, *That kid has a nicer car than I do! Gosh, I wish I wasn't in so much credit card debt!*

Parents will often ask me, "Dr. Castro, I hear what you're saying about educating our daughter Sara about money . . . contracts, delayed gratification, and all that, but I just get so confused about what I should spend on her and what is inappropriate. I don't want to overdo it, but I also don't want to deprive her."

I always respond with the question "Legally, what are the four things you must provide your kid?" Often their first answer is "Love and support." Shaking my head, I correct them. "No, as a parent living in the United States of America in this great state of Missouri, providing love and support is not a legal requirement." I sadly add that every day I see parents who don't love and support their kids to the extent that they should.

I continue. "The four things that you are legally bound to provide your kid are the following: Number 1: You must provide a roof over their heads. No yelling at your kids, 'Go to the backyard! You're in the doghouse!' (The doghouse doesn't suffice as adequate shelter.) Number 2: You must provide food. And that doesn't mean running out to McDonald's every time little Joey starts whining that he wants a Big Mac. Just having sufficient, nutritious food in the home is fine. Number 3: You must make sure your child gets an education. Public school, private school, homeschooling—it doesn't matter. But you'll get that knock on your door from a caseworker if your kid isn't learning. And finally, Number 4: You must meet basic safety and medical needs. In other words, if your kid is sick, you must get treatment. This also means that your home must be clean and nontoxic so as not to risk the health and safety of your child."

I then ask my famous rhetorical question: "Okay, besides these four basics, what else do you have to provide your kids?" I don't even wait for an answer. I yell out, "Nothing! Absolutely nothing! That's the answer!" Beyond these four essentials, everything else we give our kids is a privilege, a borrowed gift, and these things all cost money. It is not a requirement to buy your kid the new PlayStation 3 for Christmas or the iPod Nano for Hanukkah. It is a privilege to have those extravagant things, not a given.

I call these items *"borrowed gifts,"* because, by law, kids don't own anything—not even gifts! Legally, until your children are eighteen years old, you, the parent, own everything. That cool skateboard Grandma bought little Joey for his birthday? It's not Joey's skateboard, it's yours. That portable DVD player little Susie received from Aunt Betty? It's not Susie's DVD player, it's yours. And my personal favorite: that door leading into the bedroom that little Joey occupies? It's *your* door, not his! I love the look on a thirteen-year-old's face when I explain to him or her that, fundamentally, kids own nothing. It's the look of "You have got to be kidding me! I don't even own my bedroom?" Try it sometime if your teenager refuses to follow the rules in YOUR house. Take off his bedroom door. I'm serious. There is nothing that drives a teenager crazier than removing the door to his room when he defies his parents.

To some of us, the saying "Money is the root of all evil" can appear to be true. Family relationships frequently crumble around the issue of money. People's zest for life can get fiercely squeezed and drained by money problems. Especially intense bad emotions, such as anger, jealousy, resentment, rage, and fear can flare up like a brush fire when money comes into the equation. Misunderstanding and misuse of money can bring out the worst in all of us. But by Giving Room to acknowledge that money, like the strands of a multicolored woven blanket, is intertwined in all that we do in life, we grow as individuals. Don't block these monetary realities from your life. Give Room to not take money for granted. Open your mind. Slow down and Create Space to look at money seriously; don't shy away from it. Money is a powerful entity in our lives not just for its purchasing power but also for its emotional underpinnings.

It's no different for kids. Embracing the realities of "the almighty dollar" with our children gives them Room to Grow and develop through their early years. Allowing them to struggle with decisions about what to do with their money—even if it's just choosing whether to buy a SpongeBob coloring book or to save their cash—teaches them responsibility and gives them Room to Grow to develop priorities and a sense of responsibility. Introducing the concept of "contracts" in a young one's life can Give Room for a sense of accomplishment and self-determination. By showing our children how to earn, use, save, manage, and even give away money, we help prepare them for what's in store in life. And by establishing the "four things you must provide your kid," we begin the process of educating today's youth on the difference between what is truly a *need* and what is only a *want*.

PARENTING CLASS 101: BUILDING FRUSTRATION TOLERANCE

Humans are born narcissistic. Babies and young children are developmentally unable to focus on the needs of others, and that's as it should be. It is actually vital and necessary that their needs come first. Clearly, this is very different from the narcissist-masochist continuum I discussed earlier, where the narcissist's self-focus is all about getting his needs met and not caring about the negative impact it could have on others. Some of us grow out of this narcissism as we age, and some of us, to varying degrees, don't. There is nothing psychologically patho-logical or wrong about this narcissism. When we are babies, the world revolves around us, and rightfully so. It is a normal stage of development for kids to demand and receive atten-tion. When cute little redheaded Betty—all eight pounds nine ounces of her—lets out a piercing cry as she takes her first breath, her world reacts immediately with concern. The nursing staff devoted solely to Betty's well-being jumps into action. Betty's overall health is quickly evaluated. Any medical issues are addressed at once. She is bathed, swaddled in blan-kets, and, within minutes of birth, she is suckling at her mother's breast. Betty's only requirements: breathe, nurse, pee, poop, cry, and then repeat.

However, it is our job as parents, teachers, uncles, neigh-bors, psychologists, and human beings to teach kids that, as they grow and develop, "the world doesn't revolve only around *you*. Sometimes you must wait your turn." In addition to pro-viding the essentials (a safe and loving environment, nourish-ment and other materials for survival), this task of pushing kids away from the narcissistic stance of "It's all about me!" is one of the most pressing jobs for a parent or caregiver. Sometimes parents get lucky and have these extraordinary kids who seem to have an innate inclination toward genuine caring and humility. You tell them only once what to do, and, magically, they do it! They have a natural desire to help, sometimes put-ting their own needs and wants aside in the interests of others. Their inner core Gives Room to giving and is constantly being reenergized. Like a finely tuned Turbo 928 Porsche engine, these acts of cooperation and kindness become more powerful the farther along the road of life these little angels travel.

However, most of us parents are not so lucky. The narcissistic infant can easily become the selfish toddler. The bratty preschooler usually graduates to the whiney first-grader. The demanding adolescent can transform overnight into the unbearable teenager. Even our sweet little redheaded Betty, whose fiery personality used to be cute, is now an egotistical young woman. It is difficult for her to think about the needs of others, and when she doesn't get what she wants, Betty has a temper tantrum. As parents, we regard a two-year-old's temper tantrum as bad but natural; however, we never expected the devastation and ugliness generated by a twenty-two-year-old's temper tantrum. No longer is Betty just flopping around, kicking and screaming, "I want that toy! I want that toy!" When a young adult has a temper tantrum, the results can be dangerous and permanent. Often, laws are broken, drugs are consumed, and at the very least, the individual's potential is severely curtailed.

Building frustration tolerance in our kids is about Giving Room to take the time and hold them accountable for their actions. Remember, Giving Room is difficult and takes great effort. It is so much easier to wave your kid off when they misbehave, "Go to your room . . . just go." But by doing the *right* thing, not the *easy* thing, space is created for the child to grow. The way to teach kids to be kind, considerate, and humble is easy to grasp yet difficult to implement. If we want to teach our kids these values, we must first help them to build frustration tolerance. Why? Because the world is so damn frustrating! *Building frustration tolerance in a child is critical to building a mentally healthy kid.* As adults we're well aware of how frustrating the world can be. It's frustrating to work hard all week just to pay the bills. It's frustrating to sit in traffic knowing you're late for that important business meeting. It's frustrating to say no to that new pair of shoes because you have to use the money for your kid's baseball camp. It is frustrating when the air conditioner customer-service representative has you on hold for thirty minutes while the temperature in your house tops off at ninety degrees. And you know the $650 bill is soon to follow. Frustration is a big part of life—and kids must be taught to deal with it. Obviously, adults can help teach this by setting a good example themselves.

Kids pay a heavy price in life when they can't tolerate frustration. If adults don't provide them with opportunities to build a tolerance for frustration early on, the "Triple Whammy" often occurs. **Whammy 1:** *Lack of achievement occurs when one can't tolerate frustration.* Kids who are frustrated are going to find it difficult to be productive in life and so they rarely reach their potential. For example, kids struggling to complete school often find it extremely difficult to hold down a job. This is because the juggling act required in performing well in school *and* on a job can be extremely frustrating.

Consider, for example, one of my favorite family therapy cases: the Jordans. Zeke Jordan's fifth-grade science teacher, Mr. Rohan, tells him, "You must turn in your science project tomorrow, and if you don't, you will fail my class." Zeke goes home with an intellectual understanding of the steps involved in the science project and knows he can do it. He's actually had these instructions in mind for well over a month but has not yet taken any action. Still, it would be too frustrating for Zeke to spend several hours immediately after school working on the project—after all, he's just come from school and needs to unwind! He begins to rationalize: "Well, if I go bike riding with my friends for a little while, I can get to the project after dinner." Zeke is off on his bike! Next thing he knows, dinner is over and it's 7:30 p.m. Zeke's mother instructs him to take his shower and clean up his room. While putting on his pj's and kicking at the toys in his room (way too many to actually pick up and put away in one evening!), Zeke clicks on his TV. Almost instantly, he's mesmerized by the latest episode of *The Suite Life of Zack & Cody*. Remote control in hand, Zeke collapses on his bed. The show ends and a commercial comes on. The conclusion of the show triggers the thought of his not-yet-started science project, and he becomes overwhelmed. Quickly, Zeke maneuvers his way through his messy room and heads for the kitchen. Angrily, he bellows, "Mom! Why didn't you remind me about my science project?" For the next several hours, till way past midnight, Zeke and his mother do verbal battle while trying to slap together a project. Exhausted and angry, they glue on one more cardboard tree and fall into bed. The next day, Zeke receives a C on the project and an F for daily class participation—because he's fallen asleep on his desk.

Zeke had the intellect to have earned an A on the project. But his lack of frustration tolerance led to procrastinating and ultimately to underachieving. Furthermore, Zeke was flooded with intense emotions, especially when his predicament became clear to him. Unable and/or unwilling to tolerate the inevitable frustrations of planning and executing his science project in a thorough and timely way, Zeke not only received a poor grade but also suffered emotionally. This is **Whammy 2: *Lack of frustration tolerance leads to emotional instability and low self-esteem.*** If Zeke had diligently and methodically completed the steps for his project over the month allotted, he would have spared himself much emotional pain. First, while riding his bike with friends, Zeke wasn't *completely* enjoying himself. Sure, he had a good time, but there was an anxious feeling deep inside that prevented him from truly Giving Himself Room to enjoy the time with his friends. And throughout the previous month of knowing about, but trying not to think about, the dreaded project, Zeke had felt anxious and increasingly insecure.

By the final night, Zeke's anxiety had reached the breaking point. He needed to do something with his lack of confidence and worry. Therefore, he jumped into denial by losing himself in the fantasy world of his favorite TV show. Unfortunately for Zeke, like everything else in life, the show ended. This was his cue for the final emotional wave: blame. To hide from his anxiety and guilt, Zeke displaced his anger on the one person he knew would take it—good old Mom! Thus goes the vicious emotional cycle that makes up Whammy *2. Lack of frustration tolerance leads to anxiety, which leads to low self-esteem, which leads to rationalization and denial, which leads to displacement.* Then it circles back and starts all over again, always culminating in feelings of underachievement and not being "good enough."

As life moved on for Zeke, his lack of tolerance for frustration became more and more painful and debilitating. And as he avoided opportunities to responsibly experience the normal disappointments and struggles of life, Zeke's self-esteem continued to plummet, while his self-centered attitude mushroomed. The more a person suffers from low frustration tolerance, the more anxiety, disappointment, and self-doubt increase in his life. These are painful feelings to have to deal with on a daily basis. Therefore, people like Zeke tend to develop an attitude of omnipotence and grandiosity that serves to cover up their overwhelming feelings of inadequacy. This is **Whammy 3**: *The older such a person becomes, the more they suffer overwhelming feelings, and the more they convince* *themselves that they can do no wrong; everyone else is to blame. Thus, it is difficult, if not impossible, for such a person to experience truly meaningful relationships in life.*

Individuals who can't tolerate life's frustrations all seem to hold one core belief: "The world owes me something!" This certainly was the case with Zeke. Zeke continued to lack the opportunities to build a tolerance for frustration. Throughout his childhood, adolescence, and into his later teenage years, Zeke's parents constantly "took the hit" for their son, rarely allowing him to experience disappointment or frustrating feelings. For example, two weeks into Zeke's Little League baseball season, his coach reprimanded him for "slacking off" and not being ready in his position while playing shortstop. After the game, Zeke was furious! The intensity of his anger was over the top as he bad-mouthed his coach to the other players. "We have the worst coach ever! Why do you think we've lost our first two games? Because he sucks, that's why!"

On the car ride home with his parents, Zeke raved on. "That guy is such an idiot! Who is he to tell me what to do when he doesn't even know how to coach? He's just a big fat slob! No way am I ever going to play for him again!"

As always, Zeke's parents tiptoed around their son's outburst, carefully choosing words to calm him. "Now, Zeke, maybe you shouldn't say that. Don't you think the coach acts like that with all the players?"

Zeke rolled his eyes in annoyance, dismissing his parents' words with a wave of his hand. "The coach is a total idiot, and you both are idiots too if you can't see that!"

Trying to project some authority, Dad put in, "Now, Zekey, hold on! Take it easy! It just might be a good idea to give it another shot."

Zeke crossed his arms and lifted his nose. "I am not going back, period! End of conversation."

After barely graduating from high school, Zeke "lucked out" when his father was able to buy him admission into one of the local colleges by donating money to the new school library. Zeke failed four out of the five courses his first semester and was kicked out of school, even though the newly built Jordan Library bore his last name. Zeke was outraged. "This is bullshit, Dad!" he blasted. "You should get our money back!" When Zeke's friends and family asked him what happened with his studies, Zeke zeroed in on blaming "shitty teachers" and the college's lack of prestige. "That school sucked anyway," he concluded.

For a year after being expelled, Zeke lived with his parents. He occasionally worked menial jobs that his father arranged for him, only to be fired for not showing up. The familiar pattern was laid early in life: he did well on the job for about a week (just as when he was a kid in school), working hard and diligently. Then, the first time his boss asked him to do something he didn't want to do (putting Zeke in an uncomfortable situation), he became resentful. Passive aggressively, he would stroll into work late, grinning lackadaisically. Zeke would then be reprimanded for his weak work ethic. Inevitably, he'd slack off on the job and be terminated for his attitude and performance. Predictably, Zeke would either quit or be fired, but he always blamed someone else.

Zeke decided to give college another shot in beautiful Miami, Florida, yet nothing had changed. He lied to his parents, proudly giving them updates about his stellar grades and all the enriching extracurricular activities he had been participating in.

His parents were overjoyed. "Finally!" they exulted. Naturally, Zeke was lying, and his folks kept sending him cash. The truth was, he was failing miserably and getting drunk every night. The crash occurred when Zeke was arrested for public intoxication and vandalizing a fellow student's car. As they left the Miami police station, Zeke's father was confused and annoyed. "Why the hell would you bash in that girl's car windows? What the hell were you thinking?"

Zeke shrugged. "She's a bitch and it doesn't matter. Her parents are loaded. Replacing those windows is pocket change to them."

Today, three years later, Zeke continues to underachieve. A typical day for Zeke starts at 2:00 p.m., when he rouses himself for breakfast. While he eats his cereal and watches *The Price Is Right* on the kitchen TV, he dreams of being a contestant and winning a million dollars.

Zeke's mother tries to talk to him. "So, what are your plans for today, honey? Are you going to look for a job?"

Zeke doesn't answer; he just grunts.

"Oh, honey, would you mind picking up your father's clothes at the cleaners this afternoon? I would really appreciate it."

Now Zeke's ears perk up. "Sure, Mom, but I'm going to need some cash." Though the cleaning bill will be just ten dollars, Zeke is able to swindle thirty dollars out of his mom. He exits the kitchen without cleaning his cereal spills or putting the milk away. Next stop is his home entertainment center, where he'll spend several hours playing his video game Halo 2, while his four-hundred-dollar iPod blasts through his nine-hundred-dollar Bose speakers.

Hours later, Zeke's mother yells down to Zeke, "Did you pick up Daddy's clothes at the cleaners? It's 6:45, and they close in fifteen minutes."

Annoyed that his mother has interrupted him just as he is about to defeat Level 12, Zeke yells, "No, I've been busy! I'll do it tomorrow or you can do it yourself!"

At 10:30 p.m., Zeke's buddy Daniel calls. "C'mon, dude! Let's go hit the bar for *Monday Night Football.*"

At the bar, Zeke drinks twelve beers, insults four girls, takes a pee in the restroom sink, nearly gets into a barroom brawl, and drives home drunk at 3:00 a.m. And so ends another Day in the Life of Twenty-Two-Year-Old Zeke Jordan. Zeke is the poster child for parents unwilling to teach their children frustration tolerance. And you don't have to look far to find many Zeke Jordans in your own neighborhood.

When Zeke's parents came to see me, they were angry and dejected. They explained how Zeke had always been "a handful" and revealed that for the past few years he had been living in their basement, wasting his life away. During the clinical interview, Zeke's parents tried to spend a lot of our time talking about all the medications he had been on in the past for ADHD, depression, anxiety, bipolar disorder, alcohol abuse, oppositional defiant disorder (persistent pattern of tantrums, arguing, and angry or disruptive behaviors toward authority figures), and so on. Over and over, these parents wanted to focus on their son "being ill." Shaking her head, Mom remarked, "Zeke has been to so many therapists and he has been on all the different meds, but he always quits therapy. It never works, and the meds never seem to do any good."

At the end of the clinical interview during our first session, I responded to Zeke's parents as I do to all first-time clients: "I have asked you all these questions and I appreciate your thoroughness. So what questions do you have for me?"

They asked, "What would you say is Zeke's true diagnosis,

and how often do you want to see him?" I responded, "His diagnosis is *LFT*, and I don't want to see Zeke."

Confused and surprised, Mrs. Jordan asked, "LFT? What is that? And why don't you want to see our son?"

I explained, "LFT is *Low Frustration Tolerance*. It's not a true psychiatric diagnosis; I made it up. Bottom line is, your son can't handle stressful situations in life. And as for him coming in for therapy, it would be useless for him to be in therapy right now. He wouldn't get anything out of it."

Zeke's parents were clearly annoyed with me. "Well, what about all the depression and bipolar tendencies his doctors have found? What about all the damn meds? And I thought you were supposed to be an expert on teenagers and young adults! You're telling us you can't help our son?"

Calmly, I reassured Zeke's parents, "I know exactly how to help your son. What I recommend at this point is that just the two of you come in. If I can get you guys to do what I need you to do, I guarantee your son will improve."

Over the next few months, Zeke's parents were able to see how their son's lack of frustration tolerance had left him unmotivated, unproductive, and with little self-confidence. They clearly saw that Giving Zeke Room meant enforcing boundaries with their son. And they understood that Giving Themselves Room was about doing something very different than what their gut told them to do. It was time to Give Room for a new parenting style. They were able to see how Whammies 1 and 2 had negatively impacted Zeke's happiness and self-esteem. However, they were still in denial about how self-centered and selfish their son had become. They struggled with Whammy 3. They would shake their heads in disagreement. "Sure, he has trouble in stressful situations, and it makes it difficult for him to keep a job. Yes, he lacks confidence. But he really does have a good heart. He really does care about us. He does care about other people's feelings."

It took time, but Zeke's parents gradually made progress. They were able to see how not allowing their son to experience discomfort or to fail had created problems for him. Enabling Zeke to "feel okay" all the time actually hurt him. A big step came when I was able to get Zeke's parents to take the car away from him. He was drinking and driving almost every night, putting innocent lives in danger, so I finally threatened them. "My best friend and neighbor is a county cop. If that car is not taken away from Zeke by tomorrow, my buddy will be waiting to see if any drunk twenty-two-year-olds with curly red hair stroll out of West County Sports Bar next Monday night and drive away in a red Maxima."

Needless to say, they were more than a little pissed at me, but out of fear they took the car from Zeke. Zeke was aghast! "How dare you take away my car?" he yelled.

I reminded Zeke's parents, "Remember, it is your car—not Zeke's."

The dam broke five months into our work. Zeke's parents finally recognized the narcissistic monster they had created. Zeke's father said, "You are not going to believe this one. As on any typical day, our son went out drinking with his buddies. He's still angry he's not driving, but he gets rides. So last night at around 3:00 a.m., the phone rings. It's Zeke. Instantly, I think he's hurt or in trouble. I imagine he's about to tell me he's at the hospital or in jail." Mr. Jordan stops talking for several seconds and starts to tear up.

I'm concerned by his show of emotion. "Neal, what happened to Zeke?"

Shaking his head and smiling, Mr. Jordan wiped away the tears. "Nothing happened to him. When I answered the phone and inquired about his well-being, Zeke ignored my question. The only thing he said was, 'Chop-chop! I need a ride home. Get out of bed and come get me. Chop-chop!' That's when it sunk in. I couldn't believe the audacity of my son to treat me like a servant. Can you believe it? 'Chop-chop'!"

I had only one question for Zeke's father. "Did you pick him up?"

"No, no I did not," he replied, stone-faced.

That's when I gave Mr. Jordan a high five!

Children are never too young to be given opportunities to build a tolerance for frustration. For example, even infants benefit from learning how to soothe themselves by going to sleep on their own. Allowing a baby to cry, just for a little bit, is one of the first small steps we can take in providing opportunities for our kids to deal with tough situations. It's rough for a young child to learn to fall sleep on her own, but by Giving Room for the opportunity to learn, we are helping her prepare for the difficult road that lies ahead. Sure, it is appropriate to rock our baby, caressing the little body with tenderness and love. And yes, placing our little ones into the crib with their eyes still open is okay to do. Almost daily, I help parents break the habit of having to lie in bed with their ten-year-old child for two hours, just because little Malcolm doesn't feel secure going to bed on his own.

Opportunities abound for helping our kids to experience and handle frustration. Just the other day, my three-year-old daughter, Zinnia, screamed down to me from the top of the basement stairs, "Daddy, can you bring up my teddy bear? He's next to the desk."

Immediately I thought, let's build a little frustration tolerance here! I answered, "Okay, Bebop (that's her nickname). I will bring Teddy up, but it will be about a minute. You just wait there patiently." When Zinnia made the request, I was actually on my way up from the basement. But now I wanted her to experience, or sit with, the frustration of not having her teddy bear immediately. For a three-year-old, this can be just about unbearable. I turned around and began putting the wet clothes into the dryer. It took roughly seventy seconds to complete this task. Then I grabbed Teddy and headed up the stairs. I figured roughly a minute was long enough for her to wait. Zinnia was sitting cross-legged on the top stair, patiently waiting. Smiling, I handed her Teddy and said, "That was very good patience, Bebop! Very good patience! Now you go have fun with Teddy." She ran off, smiling, with Teddy tucked under her arm like a football.

A few key disciplines can help guide us adults in assisting kids to build frustration tolerance. One helpful tool is the Premack principle. Formally, the Premack principle states that more probable behaviors will reinforce less probable behaviors. I like to call it the "When-Then" method: "*When* you do the stuff that isn't fun, *then* you are allowed to do the stuff that is fun." If you live by the Premack principle, your chances for a successful life greatly increase. Giving Yourself Room as a parent by doing something difficult and against the grain (i.e., reinforcing the Premack principle) with your kids Gives Them Room to develop into humble and happy individuals.

For example, let's apply the Premack principle to little Peter. Mom tells Peter that if he wants to play with his friends, he must first complete his homework and chores. If Peter continues this pattern of behavior, he will naturally be more and more motivated to get his homework out of the way first. The opposite of the Premack principle would be Mom calling to Peter, as he throws his backpack on the kitchen floor and runs out the back door, "Okay, Petey, go have fun with your friends! Just remember that when you get back home in three hours, you really need to get to your homework!" In this scenario, Peter won't be as motivated to do his homework, because the desirable activity comes first.

Here is another example of the Premack principle. Suzie immediately attends to the six morning tasks listed on her "To-Do Board" when she wakes up. She puts on her clothes, eats breakfast, walks the dog, and so on. Then, if there is time before the bus comes, Suzie is allowed to read a book or watch some TV. The fact that Suzie gets to do something fun *after* her chores are completed reinforces these activities and makes it more likely that Suzie will continue doing them. Without such reinforcement, Suzie will sit mesmerized by an episode of *Tom and Jerry* on the kitchen TV, eating a tall stack of pancakes at a snail's pace, after which Mom will have to push her through her tasks to get ready for the bus.

Employing the Premack principle is critical to helping kids learn to tolerate frustrating situations. This "When-Then" method is indispensable in teaching youngsters how life is going to be as adults. The real world runs on the Premack principle. For example, when Ronnie turned sixteen and got his first job bagging groceries at Schnucks supermarket, his boss didn't turn to him with a smile and say, "Welcome, Ronnie, to your first day at Schnucks! Here's the freshly laundered store shirt that you'll be wearing, and here is your paycheck for the next two weeks. Good luck, enjoy your money, and now go start working!" It was understood that Ronnie needed to work two weeks and *then* he would get his first paycheck. Think about it. How successful or motivated would Ronnie have been for the first two weeks of his new job if he had gotten paid in advance? He certainly wouldn't have been as fired up to do a good job if the gratification of his paycheck were not delayed.

Parents should try to apply the Premack principle at least three times during a school day. Tell your child, "In the morning, *when* you complete your usual tasks, if there's any time left over before school, *then* you'll be allowed to do something fun. And *when* you complete your homework and chores after school, *then* you can enjoy yourself until dinner." Later in the day, you say, "After dinner you'll bathe, put on your pajamas, brush your teeth, and lay out your clothes for school tomorrow. *When* you've done these things, *then* you can watch TV until bedtime." Throughout the day, Premack's positive and predictable results are reinforcing the important life rule: Give Room to doing the stuff that isn't fun but still needs to be completed *first*, then enjoy yourself *later*. When related to the Premack principle, the impact of Giving Room is twofold: First, you are making the sacrifice, time, and effort to guide your kids to do something difficult yet rewarding. Second, by doing this, your children Create Space for positive change.

Along with using the Premack principle, parents can strengthen frustration tolerance in their kids by allowing natural consequences to unfold in a child's life. Giving Room to allow children to experience natural consequences (and not interfering in the process) is key to helping them build a tolerance for frustration. Remember Zeke quitting the baseball team because of his coach's reprimand? Had Zeke's parents *required* their son to live up to his commitment and finish out the ten-week baseball season, Zeke would have faced the natural consequences of sitting on the bench and feeling left out and alone. And if his disrespectful attitude and lack of effort had continued, Zeke would have experienced the natural consequences of getting minimal playing time and feeling isolated. Sports have a wonderful way of clearly validating natural consequences.

Allowing kids to experience natural consequences often produces *multiple* natural consequences. When this occurs, children learn even quicker that, *in life, even one action—just one slight "slip"—can have costly repercussions.* Teddy's parents felt lost when they came to see me. Teddy, a thirteen-year-old middle-schooler, was a good kid. He earned above-average grades, his friends were respectful, and he was one of the better players on the football team. Although he was self-centered, Teddy certainly fell into the "good-enough" range for a teenager. If fact, the pressing issue that brought Teddy's family to see me was simply that Teddy struggled to get himself out of bed in the morning.

The battle always began the night before. Teddy's parents would plead, "Teddy, it's 10:30 and you really need to start settling down."

Teddy would blow off his parents with something like, "Just a minute! Just let me catch the monologue on the *Tonight Show*." By 11:00, Teddy's exhausted parents would head off to bed as Teddy gradually dozed off to the drone of his TV.

Mom starts the morning wake-up routine with a sweet kiss on Teddy's forehead and a pleasant-sounding, "Hi, honey. It's 6:30. The bus will be arriving in thirty minutes. Time to get up!" On her second attempt, at 6:40, Mom's voice becomes more direct, and she gently shakes his shoulder. "It's time to get up, Teddy. Come on—let's go."

Teddy lets out an agonized groan and rolls over.

Now it's 6:47, and Mom is angry, her voice strident. "Get up now! The bus is going to be here soon, and I have an important meeting to get to! I'm not driving you today!"

Sometimes Teddy would barely catch his bus, sprinting down the street with his shoes and socks in one hand and a piece of buttered toast in the other. More often than not, however, Teddy missed the bus, and his mother was furious, knowing she'd be late for work. During the drive to school, Teddy would sit in the backseat, silent (often dozing off), as Mom berated her son about his laziness and lack of respect.

My instructions were simple. Step one was to make sure Teddy had an alarm clock. Teddy's parents both rolled their eyes. "Yeah, we tried that route before, Dr. Castro. He'll just sleep through the alarm. It doesn't work."

I countered, "Now wait a second. You two told me that one Saturday a month Teddy gets picked up at 5:00 a.m. by his friend's older brother, and all the boys drive two hours to play paintball. You mean to tell me that you guys get up at 4:45 a.m. on those Saturdays to make sure your son is up out of bed?"

Embarrassment is evident as they nervously shift on the couch. "Well, no, Dr. Castro. He is able to get himself up on those days."

I ask, "How?"

Answer: "The alarm clock."

Now that I've established that Teddy's parents have indeed supplied their son with a successful tool (a loud and annoying alarm clock) to assist him in getting up in the morning, Step Two is communicating to Teddy exactly what his responsibilities are on school mornings. His parents say, "Teddy, we are no longer going to wake you up for school. It is your responsibility to get up on your own, do the things you need to do, and get to the bus stop by 6:55. So let's talk about what time you should set your alarm so that the mornings run smoothly."

The next day, Teddy's alarm rang at 6:30 a.m. and it kept ringing for ten minutes. Finally, the alarm stopped when Teddy swatted the clock across the room, causing the electronic device to unplug. As instructed, Mom did not enter his room. She paced in the kitchen, nervously chewing on her fingernails. Then it was 6:45 a.m., and no sign of Teddy. Fifteen minutes later and still dead silence in Teddy's room . . . 7:10 a.m. . . . 7:20 a.m. . . . Though more and more worried as the minutes passed, Teddy's mother stayed the course and did not wake her son.

Suddenly Teddy burst out of his room. "What the hell is going on? It's 7:30! Why didn't you wake me up? I have that damn math test in fifteen minutes! Hurry up, we've got to go!"

Good trouper that she was, Teddy's mom followed my orders. She responded, "Teddy, you have two choices. You can call a taxi and spend ten bucks of your allowance to get to school. Or, I can drive you to school, but I'm not going to be ready for at least ten minutes, and you will have to pay me the ten bucks for the inconvenience."

Teddy was furious. Kicking the pantry door, he screamed, "What the hell is this all about?! I have to get to that math test or else Coach Bradley is going to be fuming."

Teddy's mother walked away. "Let me know if you choose to have me drive you."

Just before Mom pulled out of the driveway to drive Teddy to school, she turned to her son. "Ten dollars, please."

Disgusted, Teddy spat back, "I'll give it to you when I get home."

No longer feeling nervous, Mom didn't flinch. "I'm not driving you until you pay me the ten dollars."

"This is fucking bullshit!" Teddy erupted, storming out of the car. It wasn't long before he was back with the ten dollars.

Teddy remained silent and seething during the drive. Finally, they reached the front door of the school.

"Have a good day, honey."

Teddy didn't acknowledge his mother's kind words. He slammed the car door shut and angrily sprinted toward the entrance.

Now it was time for Mom to launch Step Three. Picking up her cell phone, she began dialing the vice principal at Teddy's school. "Yes, hello, Mr. Rosen. This is Janet Myers, and I just wanted to let you know that my son Teddy is walking into school right now. The time is exactly 8:13 a.m. Let me be very clear. I am not giving Teddy an excuse for being late today. It was his choice to be late, so I would expect you to handle this situation as you would for any student who chooses not to arrive at school on time. Thank you, and if you have any questions, feel free to give me a call."

Mr. Rosen got the message loud and clear. Teddy was given detention for the next two days for being tardy.

Ready for a quiz?

What were the natural consequences of Teddy's decision to continue sleeping?

You may be thinking, I know the answer! The natural consequences were that it cost Teddy money and time—ten dollars paid to Mom for the ride and two, hour-long detentions after school. The more expanded answer is that Teddy's choice to ignore his alarm clock and extend his sleep produced *multiple* natural consequences far surpassing the two obvious losses of time and money.

First, because he was running late that morning, Teddy suffered the natural consequence of missing breakfast. Missing this important meal led to Teddy having trouble focusing at school, feeling sluggish all day, and experiencing difficulty interacting with friends. Furthermore, although he had his lunch, Teddy was still lagging on the football field after school during practice. Inadequate nutrition and an agitated mental state prevented Teddy from reaching his potential academically, socially, and athletically.

Serving detention for being late had further natural consequences. The two days of detention forced Teddy to be late for football practice, which then led to him being benched at the big homecoming game on Friday night, even though he was the star quarterback. Because he did not play, the football team experienced the consequence of losing the game, which also led to Teddy's teammates being angry at him for letting them down.

Teddy received a D on his math test, primarily because he didn't have time to finish all the problems due to having started late. He then had to deal with the consequence of feeling tremendous anxiety, knowing that if he didn't get an A on his next test he'd be ineligible to continue on the football team due to poor grades. Fortunately, Teddy's math teacher eased the pressure by allowing him to do extra-credit work in her office after football practice. Sadly, however, the time spent working for the extra credit took away from time that Teddy would normally spend with his girlfriend, Amy. Annoyed by his lack of attention, Amy dumped Teddy, opting to date Aaron, the star running back, instead. Aaron never had issues about getting up for school on time. Teddy's one action of sleeping in led to multiple consequences: a broken heart, annoyed teammates, a frustrated coach (which led to no playing time), and a thinner wallet!

There are so many important lessons that kids need to learn in childhood! A teacher instructs Annie in her ABC's and simple addition. Erik's mom stresses the importance of good manners at the dinner table and urges him to introduce himself with a firm handshake while always looking his new acquaintance in the eye. But when I am asked by parents, "As a psychologist, what do you think is the most important thing to teach kids?" my answer invariably focuses on providing opportunities to build frustration tolerance. The extent to which an individual lacks that tolerance, that poise, that discipline, is the extent to which that person is unproductive, depressed, and bitter at the world for "turning its back" on him or her. Kids need the guidance and strength to not shy away from situations that may be difficult or uncomfortable for them. Guided by the Premack principle and supported by the instant feedback of natural consequences, we can look at the frustrating situations kids face as wonderful opportunities for them to build tolerance for the inevitable struggles in life. This is Giving Room for healthy child development.

PARENTING CLASS 101: CONSISTENCY IS THE KEY

Time for a quiz: *Which of the two kids described below do you think will be more likely to live a happy, satisfying, and emotionally stable life?*

First there is ten-year-old Anne who, on many levels, received very little from her mother. Was there food on the table and a roof over Anne's head? Yes, although dinners tended to be of the peanut butter and jelly or leftover mac and cheese variety. The two-bedroom apartment Anne and her mom lived in since her birth was in the slums of the city, and the ceiling occasionally leaked, but the heat worked in the winter and the AC kicked on during the warm months. Did Anne have enough clothes to wear? They were somewhat threadbare and certainly outdated, but she had clothes. Besides the bare necessities, though, Anne had nothing. No toys to play with unless a classmate let her borrow one. No TV or computer, though there was a TV in Mom's room, but Mom's room was out of bounds, and besides, Anne was forbidden to watch TV. Anne spent her free time working on her studies or reading the books she checked out from the school library.

Anne had no father. Her biological sperm donor dad deserted her mother shortly after Anne was born, leaving the two with little money. Mom was forced to stand in line for food stamps. Physically, Anne was the spitting image of her father, and her mother resented her for it. "What crappy luck that you look just like that son of a bitch!" she'd sometimes blurt.

Clinically depressed for years and angry at the world, Anne's mother could turn a bright summer day into a cold rainy night. When her mother did speak to her, Anne could usually predict the words—"Life sucks!" "People suck!" "God sucks!" And especially, "Men suck!" Watching her studious daughter hitting the books, Mom could be counted on to say something like, "I don't know why you study so hard, Anne. Life is going to shit on you too!"

Anne quickly learned that it was futile to challenge her mother's bleak outlook on life. She'd mastered the routine: just keep quiet, do the things you need to do, and life will move along. Sure, there would probably be no gifts at Christmas, and the start of summer break meant that Anne would have to wait three months until she was back at the place she loved most— school. But the seasons would change, and, like the sapling maple at the door of her housing complex, she would grow and mature . . . eventually she would be eighteen.

Second, there is Anne's fifth-grade classmate, Derrick. He shared some common circumstances with Anne. Derrick was also abandoned by his father, being raised primarily by his frequently depressed mom. But unlike Anne's gloomy yet predictable childhood, Derrick felt like he was on a roller coaster, never knowing what vicious jolt or sudden turn life would take next. Derrick's mother was not always the bitter, unempathic caregiver that Anne's mom was. When she was in the beginning stages of dating a new guy, or working a new and exciting job, Derrick's mom was warm and lively. She would give Derrick a bear hug as she arrived home from work, trilling, "Come here, you cutie! I want to hear all about what you did today at school!" Derrick would beam with happiness.

Unfortunately, Mom's unstable boyfriends would eventually become abusive, turning Derrick and his mom's life upside down. Not one time during the first ten years of his life did Derrick live in an apartment for more than eighteen months. By the time he was ten, Derrick had gotten the midnight shoulder-tap over half a dozen times. With a fresh black eye, Mom would sneak into Derrick's room in the middle of the night and whisper, "Be really quiet. We need to leave— now! We don't have the time or the room in your suitcase to take the toys. Just throw your clothes in. Eddy's passed out on the couch, so now is the time for us to leave."

Derrick was filled with mixed emotions as he and his mother sped down the highway in their twenty-year-old station wagon with everything they owned piled in the back. Relieved that Eddy, like all the other abusive guys who had come and gone, was now out of his and his mom's life, he felt safe. But he was also nervous about the unknown. Where would they live? Where would their next meal come from? Where would he go to school? Who would his friends be? Would there be any bullies? And then there was the scariest unknown—how long before the bottom would drop out again? Would they survive it?

We feel bad for Anne and Derrick. Life has dealt both kids a very poor hand. Both have been given the message "Be very wary about trusting others." Neither child had someone in their corner. Anne and Derrick are likely to carry the lifelong emotional baggage of not having a dad or a consistent male mentor to guide and give unconditional love and care. Because of their unfortunate childhoods, these youngsters lacked many opportunities to grow emotionally, socially, and relationally.

Back now to the original question: *Who will be more likely to live a happy, satisfying, and emotionally stable life?* Anne's childhood was certainly no picnic, but I feel more concerned about the psychological damage Derrick has suffered. This is because Anne was given one important "gift" that Derrick was deprived of. Anne was given *consistency*. Sure, that consistency was ugly, bordering on neglect, but there were no unexpected surprises popping out at Anne from around every corner. No twists and turns. She knew very clearly what she could control and what was beyond her control. Consistently, her mom communicated the message, "Look around, Anne! What you see is what you get, and it sure ain't a lot! You want something more in life? Well, it's not coming from me—so deal with it!" Like the changing of the seasons, Anne's early years were predictable.

Such was not the case for Derrick. Mixed messages swirled around his confused head daily. One day his mother would be the "good-enough mother," providing not only the essentials in life—housing, food, clothing, safety—but truly being a warm and nurturing parent. She would help Derrick with his homework, talk to her son about the dangers of drugs and alcohol, and tuck him into bed at night with a kiss on the forehead. Sadly, this storybook day could be immediately followed the next morning by Mom blowing off work and spending the rest of the day drinking two-fifths of whiskey. Sometimes, when Derrick arrived home from school, his mother would be drunk, at paranoid odds with the world. "I'm not having a good day, Derrick!" she'd wail. "You're making your own dinner tonight!" Then she'd slam her bedroom door.

Providing a structured, consistent, and predictable atmosphere for children gives them Room to Grow in an emotionally healthy manner, even when the environment is pretty ugly, as in Anne's case. Consistency promotes mentally sound minds, leaving little room for confusion.

Consider, for example, the dynamic of giving our kids *choices*. As many parents know from reading parenting books or just by trial and error, giving their children clear, reasonable choices—as opposed to just randomly telling them what to do—actually raises the likelihood of their complying with our wishes. The following scenario demonstrates a random style of parenting. Mom says, "Chris, you need to pick up those toys." Five minutes pass, and again she prompts, "Chris, come on. I would really like for you to pick up those toys!" Another five minutes, and she's starting to steam: "I really don't want to tell you again, Chris, to get to those toys!" Time ticks on, and eventually she loses it. "All right, THAT'S IT! This time you've

171

pushed me too far, young man, and for your punishment, you are NOT going to Sammy's birthday party!"

To me, that inconsistent way of parenting is bewildering and unfair. Chris never knows whether it's going to be the first, eighteenth, or forty-fifth incident that will make Mom snap and pull out a draconian punishment. Giving her son a choice will go a long way toward fostering consistency and mental health for little Chris. Here is a much better way to address the situation: Mom positions herself between the TV and Chris, ensuring that her son makes eye contact with her. She says calmly, "I need to let you know that those toys (she points) in the corner need to be picked up and put in this (pointing again) toy basket. Then the basket needs to be put on this (pointing again) shelf. I want this to be done immediately. If it is not done immediately, you will not be going to Sammy's birthday party on Friday night."

This is a better approach because it is specific and measurable, which supports consistent parenting and fosters a more trusting view of people. Chris clearly understands the rules and the consequences of disobeying them. Toys in basket means toys in basket. Immediately means immediately. Party on Friday night means party on Friday night. Also, you can see in this example an absence of exclamation marks. There was little emotion in Mom's voice as she explained the choice.

I often tell parents, "When you are giving a choice to your kid that is specific and measurable, take the emotion out of your words just as you would if you were asking the question (giving the choice), "What flavor ice cream would you prefer, chocolate or vanilla?" There is not much emotion in such a question. It is what it is.

Frequently, parents comment, "But isn't that kind of strict

to threaten, *Do it or else?*" There is nothing inherently strict about giving your child a choice. Certainly, some choices may seem stricter or harder to make than others, yet the gift of giving choices actually decreases kids' worries because there are no surprises about how Mom or Dad are going to parent and what is "coming down."

Also, you may have noticed in my example that after Mom makes sure she has Chris's full attention by making eye contact, she starts off by saying, *"I need to let you know."* This phrase is very helpful to parents. It enables them to get right to the "choice." Too often, parents will dance around, trying to get their words out. They use way too many words with their kids: *"Um, Chris, ah, yeah, ah . . . I really need to ask a favor and it's not going to take that long, but you really need to listen because it looks to your mother and me that you've been watching that TV long enough, and it's important that at least sometimes you help around here because you are part of the family! So I would really appreciate . . . blah, blah, blah."* That's sixty-five words! I will snap at parents, "Enough already! Stop dancing! It's like the music is playing and you two are waltzing all over the house. Just start off by saying, *'I need to let you know,'* and then give the choice. After that, imagine me telling you to zip your mouth shut—and walk away from your child!"

Providing kids choices that are clear, measurable, unemotional, and not too wordy, is Step One to consistent parenting. Yet even more important than the choice is our follow-through on whatever choice the child makes. Back to our example! Chris clearly understands the choice being given, yet shoos his mom away from the TV and grouses, "Hey! I'm watching my show now, Mom! Leave me alone!"

The next day Chris questions his mom about the party.

"Mom, am I going to Sammy's party right after school on Friday or should I come home first to change?"

Mom replies, "You are not going to Sammy's birthday party because you chose to not pick up your toys when I asked you to."

The following day is Thursday evening, and Chris is pleading, "Mom, please! I'll be extra good this weekend. I'll even clean the entire basement! I really want to go! All my friends will be there!"

Mom holds her ground. "No."

And then comes Friday afternoon, and Chris is in tears. "Mom, everyone is going to hate me if I don't go. I'll do anything to make it up! Anything!"

Then Mom does what all parents have done at some point. She gives in. "All right, Chris. But I am telling you, next time . . ."

By giving in, Mom has just reinforced that her words mean *nothing*! When I tell this to parents, they'll often give me a hurt look, as if I were being mean to them! But this is reality, folks! Simple behavioral theory proves it. Choices and natural consequences mean nothing if we are not willing to follow through. Truth is, I would rather see parents let their kids run wild with very few rules than for them to be constantly making hollow threats that they never follow through on. Not following though on your words exacerbates bad behavior and emotional instability.

The problem with good consistent parenting is that it is *very hard work*! It is so much easier to just brush things off with "Well, we'll see! But if I let you go to the movies, you'll have to promise me that next time you'll . . ." It's tremendously hard work—a labor of love—to give really good and fair choices, and then to follow through. If a parenting principle is truly a good one, then get ready! To implement any strong and time-proven principle is going to take work.

The Premack principle that we discussed earlier can be your rudder to navigating these turbulent waters. Adam's mother came to see me about one major issue she had with her son. Adam refused to do his homework before he watched TV. Mom explained, "Overall, Adam is a good kid, getting good grades and staying out of trouble. But what ends up happening, Dr. Castro, is that he won't start his homework until 10:00 p.m., and it often turns into such a battle." After going over the "When-Then" method with Mom, she is ready to give it a shot. But the following week she returns and says, "It didn't work. I unplugged the TV and told him it was not going on until homework was complete, but then I had to run into the kitchen to shut off the oven and sure enough, he plugged it back in and started watching!"

I explained to Mom that she'd have to brace herself for some really hard work and that if she was truly going to put in the work, Adam's behavior would likely worsen in the beginning. A week later she was back in my office, shaking her head. "Well, still no luck, Dr. C. Adam dug his heels in. This time I unplugged the TV and stuck it in the closet. And you know what? That damn kid, in the middle of the night, snuck into the closet and took the TV down and watched it all night!" Mom relayed a similar story the following week. "Okay, instead of sticking the TV in the closet, I switched strategies, as you suggested, and put it in the trunk of my car." Dejected, Mom whimpered, "Adam then snuck into my purse, got the keys to my car, removed the TV again while we were sleeping, and watched it all night!"

Like a soccer team that's been pounded 5–0 by halftime, Mom, dark bags under her eyes, was ready to give up. I can always recognize the parents who are really doing the tough parenting work that I preach—they come in looking exhausted. Encouraged, I enthusiastically coached, "You are almost there! I'm telling you, the wall is almost solid. Soon Adam will not be able to break it down." The next week Mom was smiling with joy as she told the story. "OK, so I took the TV and stuck it back into the trunk of my car. Then I took my car keys and tied them around my neck. And then I went to bed."

I asked, "So what did Adam do?"

Thrilled, Mom said, "He had a temper tantrum for three days straight—kicking and screaming, throwing his body all over the ground! But then after three days he broke. He walked into the kitchen, sat down at the table, and nonchalantly said, 'I guess I have to do my homework before I watch TV.'"

This true story shows the power of the Premack principle as well as illustrating, through Adam's stubbornness and Mom's persistence, that being a consistent and loving parent takes a hell of a lot of work! But in the end, life becomes much easier. Once Adam finally "broke," the midnight battles ceased. Furthermore, Adam's personality was no longer so emotional. He knew the routine (homework first and TV after) and never questioned it. Through hard work and persistence, Adam turned into a calmer and more humble child.

This concept is nothing new. Good parenting starts with consistency. When one visits the Self-Help/Parenting section of any large bookstore, one comes upon many books and tapes emphasizing the importance of parental consistency. The message "Do what you say you are going to do!" is included in all of them. But this timeworn concept bears repeating to show that good, consistent, follow-through parenting is hard work! The reason so many of us are not consistent and struggle with follow-through is that it takes much physical and emotional effort to really do it right. One little statement like "You must do your homework before watching TV" may lead to a myriad of ugly tirades and sleepless nights if you truly intend to see results. By using the Premack principle to emphasize the importance of taking care of responsibilities before doing the fun stuff and by giving kids choices that are unequivocal, unemotional, and not too wordy, we clear a path along the initially rocky road of life to Give Room to our kids to learn about responsibility and self-respect.

PARENTING CLASS 101: SPANKINGS OR TIME-OUTS?

When parents report that their typical method of discipline is to spank their kids, most therapists kind of freak out and turn into heartless investigators. Shifting in her leather chair, Dr. Smith positions for the attack as she questions her clients about the severity of their corporal punishment. With a stern, penetrating eye, she interrogates, "So, you say you spank. Do you spank little Allison with an open hand or a closed fist? Now I need to know, do you strike Allison on any other parts of her body besides her bottom, and are marks left from your spankings? And kindly tell me, do you spank her bare flesh or over her garments?" All of a sudden, these parents, who came in seeking help, feel like there's an interrogation lamp overhead, blinding their eyes, as "detective doctor" hammers them with question after question.

In any self-help book on parenting issues, there most definitely should be a section on spanking. Needless to say, I don't blame my colleagues about questioning their patients when there appears to be a possibility of child abuse. By law, psychologists are mandated to report any signs of abuse. I have my own set of questions to rattle off when I suspect mistreatment, and there have been several times throughout my career that I have made the call to the Missouri Department of Social Services. It's not my job to determine if abuse has actually occurred, but it is my duty to report that the possibility of abuse is present.

When I learn that parents are spankers, I'm extremely careful not to put them on the defensive. They might start out by saying, "Dr. Castro, I know you probably don't agree, but sometimes Billy is so rude and defiant that a little swat on the butt is the only thing that gets his attention." I also encounter many parents who tell me that a quick spank is the only way they can think of to teach their toddlers not to run out into the street. I can empathize with these parents, as I am sure many of you parents out there can, as well. Our kids have such an amazing ability to know exactly what buttons to push and when to push them. Over and over again we tell our kids, "Just stop!" but they don't. Impulsively, we strike. Once I have determined that abuse has not occurred and that the impulsive act is more of the "harmless spanking" variety (although some people do consider "harmless" or "typical" spankings a form of abuse), I communicate to the parents that I understand and feel their frustration. Most parents are riddled with guilt for spanking their kids. Unfortunately, this can lead to inconsistent parenting. Having spanked their child, Mom and Dad now feel they must "make it up" to him by apologizing several times for their off-the-handle behavior and then taking the kid out for ice cream! These mixed messages—"Stop! Stop! Stop!" *Smack*! "Oops! I'm sorry! Time for a reward!"—leave the child confused.

However, there are parents who have no problem spanking their kids. These parents are "old school" and have the attitude that "tough love" starts with fear. There is no doubt or worry on these parents' faces when they describe the spankings to me. There is no concern that their form of discipline might cross the line of technically being abuse, and there certainly don't appear to be any feelings of guilt after the spankings. To these parents I pose the question: "Now, Dad, when you were a kid, did you ever get spanked?"

Nodding, Dad says, "You bet I did! I can remember to this day my dad walking into his closet and pulling out that four-inch-thick belt. Boy, did my butt sting for days!"

Then I will ask Dad the all-important question: "What was it that you did wrong that warranted the beating?"

Nine times out of ten, parents will respond to this question with no real answer. "Uh, I'm sure I did something pretty bad, but boy, do I remember those swats!"

I won't let Dad off the hook just yet. "Yeah, I got that part about your father giving it to you pretty good, but what I don't understand is, what did you do that was so wrong? And what behavior did you learn to do, or not do? In other words, what lesson did that belt deliver?"

Predictably, the answer is "I can't remember."

This is one major reason I advise parents *not* to use corporal punishment as a form of discipline. It might work in the short-term, but it doesn't *stick*. Sure, you can get little Billy to stop tripping his baby sister by sticking out your own leg, pushing him to the ground, and saying, "See? Now how does

179

that feel? It doesn't feel so good when it happens to you, does it?" But Billy isn't internalizing that "hitting is wrong" and he certainly hasn't learned that hurting people is wrong! He is crying, lying on the floor, scared and angry. Out of fear, his negative behavior stops for a while. Yet his anger builds, and eventually Billy lashes out again at his sister. In the future, Billy will not remember why his dad threw him to the ground. He will only remember Dad's furious look, forceful shove, and cutting words. No learning, parenting, or mentoring was achieved. "Fear" was the only reason Billy's behavior temporarily changed.

Another reason one should not spank is that it suggests to children that to change a person's behavior, physical aggression is needed. This is certainly something we don't want to model for kids. It pushes them away from "using their words" as a tool for conflict resolution. Using physical aggression as a form of discipline doesn't Give Room for children to communicate their emotionally laden needs in a healthy, nonthreatening manner. Bottom line: spankings communicate to kids that physical force will get you what you want. Sadly, no helpful lesson is imparted.

Just as in politics, with its far-left liberals and far-right conservatives, the "spanking parents" are at one extreme, and the "time-out parents" are at the other. The spanking parents will argue, "Time-outs don't work! Freddy never stays in his room when we send him there, and once he gets out he goes right back to bugging his little sister."

As a therapist and parent, I am a fan of time-outs. The problem is that many parents don't know how to execute the proper steps in implementing a time-out. First, the location of the time-out may be poor if it serves as a reinforcing environment for the kid. For example, third-grade teacher Ms. Halloway has reached her limit with eight-year-old Erik, who is disrupting her class. She explodes, "That's IT, Erik! I've had enough! Get in the hallway!"

Unfortunately, Erik doesn't mind sitting in a chair in the hallway because his two best friends have asked Ms. Halloway if they could be excused for a bathroom break. Now Erik's buddies are entertaining him by running up and down the hallway! Cheering them on from his chair, Erik quickly forgets why he is in the hallway in the first place.

Another horrible place to sentence a kid for time-out is in their bedroom. There is so much to look at and do in a kid's bedroom. In her room, the child can read books, color pictures, look at posters on the wall, pet the hamster, play dress-up, watch TV, play the PlayStation Portable, and so on. Even looking out her bedroom window at the bright red cardinal chirping in the tree can be quite pleasing to an eight-year-old.

Where should a time-out be held? A place where there is nothing! Probably the two most popular sites in a home for a time-out would be the stairs or a guestroom. The goal is that the child be in a place that is not at all entertaining. No pictures to look at, no toys to play with, and no windows to look out of. At this point, the child is in a really boring place where his mind is not distracted by engaging things. All he can do is think about why he is in time-out, how long he will be there, and how he can change his behavior to avoid a time-out in the future.

So now that we have addressed one of the major mistakes parents make when implementing time-outs—inappropriate location—it is time to explain to the child the rules of time-out. Not going over the rules is the second major mistake parents often make. Rule 1: The child must stay seated throughout the time-out. Rule 2: There is no talking. Rule 3: There is a time limit on the time-out. However, if the child breaks rule 1 or rule 2 during the time-out, the duration of the punishment will be extended. I know what many of you are thinking— "Oh, yeah, that sounds great, Dr. Castro. But it's a little harder than just laying down rules 1, 2, and 3. He will scream and bang on the stair door. We bought a cooking timer to show him how much time is left, but he just freaks out!"

Remember, folks, parenting is hard work! There will be times when your child is in time-out for quite a while, and the screaming and temper tantrums will disrupt the entire household. But as we discussed earlier, the key word is consistency. If you stick to your guns, eventually the child will break and comply with the time-out.

Another major principle for parents to remember when implementing a time-out is "Engagement vs. Disengagement." When a child exhibits positive or neutral behavior, we are inclined to engage with the child. Here is a good example of how to engage with your child: Your daughter Sally brings home an A on her spelling test *and* tells you that she has made a new friend at school. When you hear positive things like this, I suggest that you stop what you're doing, kneel down to eye level with your child, and start engaging! "Wow, Sally, you actually spelled all the words right! Some of those words look really hard! So tell me how Ms. Wright went through giving a spelling test. Did you feel nervous? And what did it feel like when she handed it back and you saw that big smiley face sticker on top of the page?" And then, "A new friend?! That's wonderful, Sally! So tell me all about your new friend. What's her name? What do you two like to do together? Maybe she can come over for a playdate this weekend." (Needless to say, you'll wait for full responses to your questions and reactions before moving on to others. If you don't pay close attention to your child's responses, your enthusiasm will not engage and will come off as false.) Sally has your full attention because she's earned and attracted it through her behavior. You are communicating your approval, interest, and natural enthusiasm to Sally through your efforts to connect. You are engaging each other—"dancing" in a healthy sea of words.

But when the behavior is negative, it is time to disengage. Force yourself to use as few words as possible and to speak with little emotion, even if you have to fake it. For example, Billy is placed in time-out for not shutting off the TV when Mom instructed, "TV off now." At this point, Mom's goal is to get Billy in the time-out using as few words as possible, then to disengage from the scene.

I explain to parents, "This is not the time to teach, mentor, explain, or advise. Just give the time-out and isolate your child for the duration of the time-out. Pretend he doesn't exist!" Sure, providing words of guidance to our children is a vital part of parenting, but there is a time and a place for it. I tell parents that once the storm has passed and the child is in an even-tempered state of mind, then they can do all the teaching they want. However, I believe it is even better to wait for the child to initiate discussion. More often than not, an explanation to your child about why he or she was in time-out is not necessary. Most kids are smarter than you might suppose. Billy knows he should shut off the TV and listen to his mother. But he's a kid and he wants what he wants. And that's okay! If the child wants to talk about the punishment later, when emotions have settled, certainly feel free to engage.

For example, you are tucking little Billy into bed, and he says, "Mommy, I just don't know why I was in time-out for forty-five minutes today. It makes me sad to think about it. And why didn't you come talk to me when I was calling for you?" This is the time to connect with your child on an emotional level about the important lesson in life: *When an authority figure asks you to do something that you know you should do, immediately do it!*

Throughout this section, and in the previous parenting sections, I have acknowledged that kids can be extremely difficult when parents try to curb negative behavior. So let me say again: It's hard work! It is maybe the hardest work we'll ever do! I know, because I'm a parent with three kids. And it's just as hard for me to apply what I get paid to teach you. Kids will fight when they want their way, pushing parents to the point of literally pulling out their hair. Some parents will do all the right things when it comes to consistent parenting. These caring parents will follow the correct steps for time-outs, they will look for opportunities to build their kids' tolerance for frustration, and they are diligent in seeking ways to teach their young ones how money impacts their lives. Yet some kids still continue to push the envelope and cross the line, exhibiting grossly inappropriate behavior. For some parents, it doesn't matter how hard they follow the traditional precepts of good, consistent parenting; like a tidal wave, these kids can be unstoppable and destructive.

Therefore, let's finish up parenting issues with a seemingly crazy topic: "The Four Reasons You Would Call the Police on Your Kids."

Now calm down and take a deep breath. I know some of you parents are thinking, *What the hell is wrong with this guy?!*

I would *never* call the police on my kid! Could you imagine all my neighbors gawking out their windows, wondering what the hell is going on?

I can certainly empathize, but I will also be very direct in telling you that it's not my concern what anyone else thinks. It is my job, first and foremost, to keep your child and your family safe.

Trust me, I've worked with many parents who have lost control of their kids. My "Four Reasons" list has helped these parents not only gain back control but has also led to Creating Space for harmony in the home.

1. *Call the police if your son or daughter physically harms himself or herself or someone else in the family.* It is illegal in the United States to physically assault someone, even if you are a minor. A spanking on the bottom that leaves no mark is legal, although not encouraged. Physically lashing out at another human being is against the law. This includes what one might consider a minor offense, such as little Joey punching his sister Betty in the arm as he passes her in the hallway. It also includes more serious offenses, such as Joey pinning his sister down and delivering several vicious blows to her head. I tell parents, "Try not to think about the severity of the physical behavior; when it comes to physical assault, I want you to think black and white—did it or did it not occur?"

2. *Call the police if your child damages your property.* It is illegal for anyone in the United States—even a minor— to damage someone else's property. And remember, you own everything in your home until your child is eigh-

CREATING SPACE FOR HAPPINESS

teen. Therefore, if Dawn, during a fit of not getting what she wants, picks up the Xbox 360 that you got her for Christmas and tosses it into the wall, producing a ten-by-ten-inch crater in the drywall and shattering the gaming system, you should call the police. "Yes, officer, I need you to come immediately. My daughter has deliberately damaged two of my things. She was so angry she destroyed my Xbox 360 and she damaged my wall."

3. *Call the police if your child runs away.* It is illegal in the United States for a minor to run away. Therefore, if Brian, your fourteen-year-old son, threatens, "Screw both of you! You can't make me clean my room! I don't have to stay here!" you need to let him know that you will be calling the police because it is illegal for him to run away. If Brian actually does run away, you better make sure to call the police, not only for Brian's safety but your own as well.

   For example, let's say Brian storms out of the house screaming, "I'm never coming back!"

   You are so frustrated with your disrespectful son that you yell back, "Good! Leave! Let's see how well you do on your own!"

   After three days of letting Brian experience the tough realities of jumping from friend's house to friend's house, wearing the same dirty clothes, you begin to wonder how much longer Brian can take not having his warm bed and forty-six-inch TV. On the fifth day, the police come knocking at your door with devastating news. Brian and his friend Aaron stole a bottle of whiskey from the convenience store. They immediately got drunk and decided

186

to steal a car. Brian was behind the wheel, swerving down the two-lane highway, when he lost control of the car and crossed the median. A sixty-mile-per-hour head-on collision ensued with a minivan filled with five kids and their parents. Everyone involved in the crash died except for the dad. Besides the trauma of losing your son, you now have the burden of finding a top criminal attorney to defend you against charges of second-degree murder. A phone call to the police letting them know your son had run away could have prevented this horrible scenario. It may sound far-fetched, but this stuff happens to people like you and me.

4. *You should call the police if your child is concealing street drugs in your home or in your car.* It is illegal in the United States, no matter how old you are, to possess illegal drugs. If the police search your car or your house and find drugs (and you did not report your child's drug use to the police), you will likely be charged with possession of and possibly intent to distribute drugs. Trust me, if the authorities find an ounce of marijuana in your house that is broken up into four quarter bags and a scale, you are in a boatload of trouble!

These four offenses—physical assault, destruction of property, running away, and illegal drugs—are not for parents to handle. This is one reason we pay taxes to fund the police department. Citizens are not equipped to handle crimes of this magnitude. If we try to restrain a child who is physically out of control, we or the child may get injured. If we allow our child to damage things in the home without notifying the police, the child will not truly know the severity of his actions. If we don't intervene when a child runs away or is using/selling drugs, we are risking the physical, emotional, and financial well-being of everyone in the family. Plus, we do our children a huge service by Giving Them Room to see that the above-mentioned severe behaviors will not be tolerated. If your child engages in any of these dangerous behaviors, it is more effective to call the police than try to settle it by yourself. A police officer saying, "Come here, son! I need to talk to you about being respectful to your parents," can have a powerful impact on a son or daughter who misbehaves. Being sent to juvenile hall (kiddie jail) for forty-eight hours quickly teaches a child that his actions have consequences. Trust me, if you don't Give Them Room to learn this when they're fourteen, society will teach them when they turn eighteen. And remember, it is a lot easier to change when you are fourteen than when you are eighteen.

In sum, I know that at times parents become so frustrated with their kids that impulsively, they want to give them a smack and yell, "Cool it!" And if they do deliver a blow, it usually works; the child complies. Unfortunately, the good behavior is short-lived, and the child reverts to defying them. Soon, the spank or the tap or the smack needs to be a little more forceful, and the scream a little louder, to achieve the desired behavior. Staying away from corporal punishment, such as spankings and more serious physical harm, and Giving Room to the proper steps to implementing a time-out is much more effective in eliciting permanent behavior and attitude change in a child. This Creates Space for the child to mature and demonstrates that using your words is the way to help people change.

But sometimes our children's behavior may be beyond our control. It is a fact of life that there might come a time when we can no longer handle an intense situation. Calling in support, such as the police, should be considered a gift to your children that will teach them right from wrong and maybe even save their life.

HOLLY'S STORY: "THERE'S NO PLACE LIKE HOME"

Katie's rhythmic breathing helped her to sleep soundly on her big sister's lap. Drool from her lower lip dripped onto Holly's knee. As the hours passed, the bumps of the ride would startle Katie, and her eyes would pop open. Holly gently stroked her sister's long blonde hair and whispered, "It's okay, Katie. Close your eyes, it's okay." Both girls wore shorts, sandals, and sleeveless shirts, yet the humidity of this Midwestern summer day had them dripping in sweat. They knew there would be no air conditioning on the Greyhound bus and that the trip would be very long. But the fare was cheap, and the girls felt at peace.

Holly gazed out the slightly opened window as the breeze brushed her hair back. Mesmerized by the rolling hills and farmland, she especially loved seeing the cows grazing in the fields. Holly loved all animals, but cows were her favorites. This past fifth-grade school year, Holly had been assigned to write a paper on an animal and she picked the cow. In her report she talked about the giving nature of cows. She was intrigued by their docile personalities and social instincts. They traveled in packs as a family, rarely venturing off alone. Cows stick together, knowing there is safety in numbers. Interestingly, when a cow is sick it instinctively departs from the herd and isolates itself, often dying a lonely death but very careful not to disturb its siblings. Holly also felt that the reality of just one cow sacrificed for the nourishment of over one hundred humans elevated this living being to sacred ground. She started her report with "The cow—such a giver."

Throughout the twenty-hour bus ride, Holly was excited, yet calm. She had not visited Grandpa McDevin in over four years. Finally she would be back on the Wisconsin dairy farm, this time with Katie, for the entire summer. It was hard work living on the farm with the 4:45 a.m. rooster wake-up calls. Once awake, the girls would milk the cows for two hours before breakfast. Holly assured Katie that she wouldn't mind the work and that they would quickly fall into the daily routine. Grandma McDevin had died before the girls were born, and Grandpa had been solely tending to the farm duties. The extra hands, albeit little, would be much-needed help this summer.

"How much longer?" Katie asked, through partially open eyes.

"We've got three more hours. Close your eyes again. That's a good girl. . . ."

Katie gently drifted back into sleep. As Holly continued to look out the window for the last few hours of the trip, her mind moved back to the past several years. She let her mind go as she relived the madness. One word described Holly's young life so far: Unpredictable.

Holly's first-grade year began when she returned from the farm, only to learn that her mother had been hospitalized. First- and second-grade years turned out to be what Holly called "The Hospitalization Years." Mommy had spent three separate ten-day hospitalizations at Philadelphia General in the psychiatric unit by the time the holidays arrived.

On Christmas Eve, the two girls snuggled in Holly's bed and prayed together. Holly enthusiastically explained to her three-year-old sister, "Katie, this is a very special night. Not only can we pray to Jesus, but we can also talk to Santa through our prayers. So what is it, Katie? What is it you want to ask for?!"

Katie said shyly, "You first, Holly, What is it you want?"

"Well, I want Santa to bring me books tomorrow (Holly had peeked in Mom's closet and found three science books she knew she would be receiving in the morning). And as for Jesus . . . Jesus, I pray that you give me the opportunity to learn a lot in school for the rest of the year. I also pray that it snows soon! Because I love the snow!" She turned to her sister. "Your turn, Katie. What is it you want to pray for?"

"Dear Jesus and Santa, I don't really care which one of you gets me this, but if one or both of you could make sure that Mommy will not go away to the hospital again, I would be so happy. Please promise me that she won't leave us again."

Holly's heart sank and she became agitated. "I don't think that is something Jesus, Santa, or both of them together can promise, Katie."

Katie argued, "But that is what I want!"

"What about toys?" Holly pleaded.

Katie's voice rose. "I don't want any toys! I want Mommy not to leave!"

Sadly, her wish was not granted, her prayers were not heard. By the end of the school year, Mommy had been back in the hospital another two times. The following school year, another four hospitalizations. Despite her tender age, Holly could hold down the daily household duties, but the devastating emotional tug-of-war she experienced when Mom needed intensive psychiatric assistance was sheer torture. The pattern was this:

First, Mommy would be full of life for a few weeks. During this manic period, she would party late into the night with friends. Or Mommy could often be found snuggling in bed with the girls, reading book after book. The girls were also apt to find their mother cleaning the apartment—incessantly. She would talk very fast, and her facial expressions would be alive with joy, yet she could also quickly become irritated. The girls loved story time at night with Mommy's lively presentations, but Holly felt the nerves tightening in her stomach, knowing that any day the bottom would drop out. Again. It wasn't a question of "if"—it was a question of "when."

When Mommy finally crashed, she crashed hard. She would not show up for work and would lock herself in her bedroom. The girls would plead as they banged their small fists on her door, "Mommy, please unlock the door. We want to talk to you!"

Holly would cry, "Mommy I made you some dinner; you need to eat something."

Sometimes Mommy would open the door and accept the food with a warm smile. Other times she would yell, "Leave me alone!" And yet other times something even worse would happen: *Silence.*

Holly made up the "Three-day Silence Rule." If Mommy did not speak or leave her bedroom for three full days, Holly would call the police. She dreaded making the call. She knew once the call was made, Mommy would be gone for weeks. But she was also aware that the lack of nutrition Mommy was experiencing could result in major medical complications. She had no choice once the seventy-two-hour time limit had passed. And where would the girls go once Mommy was in lockdown? The answer was: Wherever and whenever. Maybe two days at a distant aunt's house, where the girls would likely be picked on by their older cousins. Perhaps three days with their little old widowed neighbor, Ms. Hazelten, who was sweet as pie and would play board games with the two girls. Then possibly Holly and Katie would be yanked in another direction and forced to live in a foster home with several other homeless kids. One would think, after the pattern of neglect and uncertainty had continued long enough, that their mother would lose her rights to the girls. It never happened. Mommy was smart and manipulative. Holly also learned her first lesson about "the system": it takes a heck of a lot of damage before the state will take kids away from their homes.

Holly termed the time period from third through fifth grade as "The Moving Days." In this three-year span, the girls and Mommy moved six times. Tears of sadness and fear would trickle down the girls' faces as Mommy would wake them up in the middle of the night and instruct, "Here are a couple of trash bags. Throw as much stuff into them as you can and get outside to the car as fast as you can. We have to go—now."

The departures always had to do with Mommy running away from someone or something: boyfriend, creditor, work, landlord, police, and so on. The drill was always the same. They would leave in the middle of the night, and the escape would be swift and clean. Holly would be sad knowing she would likely never see her friends again. But even worse than the melancholy feelings was the fear. Holly would worry, "Am I going to have a roof over my head or are we going to live out of the car for a while?" "When and how will I get my next meal?" Nothing was certain or predictable. Holly felt like a pinball, randomly bounced around and knowing that at any time she could slip down the hole and the game would end.

The bus driver announced, "Next stop is in ten minutes: Madison Wisconsin Station."

Smiling, Holly looked down at Katie, who was still sound asleep. She again began stroking her sister's hair. Holly thought, *Well, at least this past year has been a little better.* No hospitalizations or moves in the past several months. The girls' mother had finally accepted the idea that taking her medication consistently was a good thing. Holly was like a drill sergeant ordering her mother to swallow the pills. She was thrilled when Mommy's psychiatrist instructed her to call him immediately if their mother stopped taking the meds. Holly felt he was the best doctor ever because of his direct, no-nonsense approach. It was obvious that all the others didn't really want to put in the time and effort to help Mommy. It enraged her that they just didn't want to be bothered. But Dr. Horn was different. He'd tilt his head down, peer over his bifocals at her, and instruct, "If she stops taking these meds, or refuses to take them, you call this number at once."

Holly thought, Can this really be true? Is there finally someone in our lives who really cares? Is there finally someone who's going to help Mommy stay well and to really love and take care of us? Is our consistently inconsistent crazy world really going to turn into a happy and normal one, just like in all those fun stories I read? Holly had her doubts. Sure, it was a good start. Several months was quite a long time for Holly's world not to wobble or crash, but she knew that with or without the meds, Mommy could shift like the wind and change directions at any moment. Desperate for some stability, Holly was excited knowing they'd be on the farm for the next three months. Her vacation had arrived. But then what? Yes, Holly had her doubts. While only ten, she'd learned that there are no guarantees in life. The real world was harsh. The first time she'd seen *The Wizard of Oz*, she'd lamented, "Boy, is that the truth! There really is no place like home."

GIVING COUPLES ROOM

Several years ago, a young couple in distress came to see me. Susan and Patrick had just celebrated their fifth wedding anniversary. They had met in college and fell in love. Immediately following graduation, they moved in together, and two years later they married. During the first few years of married life, Patrick worked a steady professional job, slowly climbing the corporate ladder. Susan was in nursing school. They had decided to hold off starting a family until Susan completed school. On the weekends, Patrick usually played golf with his college buddies, and Susan spent her time studying or exercising with her best friend. They enjoyed their evenings together watching TV dramas such as *ER* and *The West Wing*, while eating Chinese takeout. Life was busy those first few years, but the couple felt settled and satisfied. They even got a cat and named her Ms. President.

But now, entering their sixth year of marriage, they felt disconnected from each other. Susan explained, "It's not like things are horrible between Patrick and me. It's just that I feel we are growing apart. We used to do things together like taking walks, going to the movies, or just playing cards. Now it's like we're living two separate lives."

Patrick chimed in, "Yeah. I mean, we do love each other. But it's like not much is there. Plus, we argue way more than we used to."

I decide to get a baseline assessment and ask, "Okay, guys, on a scale of one to ten, how would you rank your marriage? A ten means that you feel your marriage is the best and couldn't be any better. A one would mean that you're looking, behind your partner's back, of course, for a divorce attorney. A five is somewhere in between. So take a few seconds and try to come up with the number in your head. Okay, who is brave enough to go first and give me a number?"

Couples are understandably uncomfortable when I ask this question, but usually I can get them to give me a number. Nervously, Susan and Patrick look at each other and say, "Maybe a four, or somewhere around there? Yeah, around a four." They nod in agreement.

I then ask, "And what do you imagine would help raise that number to a seven or an eight?"

Like so many couples before them, they respond, "I don't know."

So I follow up, "Well, what are you hoping to accomplish in therapy? What are your goals?"

Again, they are lost, but Patrick manages to respond, "I just think we want to save our marriage. It feels like it's slipping away." And so begins the work of couple's therapy.

Patrick and Susan's situation is not uncommon. Most people believe there needs to be some definite, definable *input* that poisons an intimate relationship. They say, "Our marriage sucks because that son of a bitch is a raging alcoholic" or "She had an affair and I just don't know if I can ever forgive her." Certainly, many of the couples who come to see me state that one of the partners "is the problem." In my experience, it is the wife who has forced the husband into couple's work. Most husbands don't have a problem letting you know they were coerced into coming to therapy. He'll say, "I'm not perfect, but I don't feel I have many problems. And the marriage is just fine for me. It's her issue, not mine." Or the male partner will communicate loud and clear that he really doesn't want to be in therapy. He'll use nonverbal behavior, such as rolling his eyes when his wife speaks or putting his hand over his mouth as if to keep himself from speaking. The rolling of the eyes, by either husband or wife, when their partner speaks, is one of those "red-hot" signals to me that the couple is disconnected and no longer in each other's corner. They have lost a key ingredient to a happy, lifelong partnership: respect for each other.

Sure, many couples enter into therapy to fix a particular issue. But just as often, I treat couples like Patrick and Susan, who really can't put a finger on why they are disconnected; they just know that they are. In these situations, I will first search with a keen eye to make sure there are no big hidden issues or events that led them to come see me. I may even request to speak with the individuals separately. In the absence of one partner, the other is likely to open up about an issue that's really driving a wedge in their relationship. This is typically the case if the issue has to do with an affair or a sexual problem. If a big issue exists, it has to be addressed in the couple's work. I don't allow silent elephants into the therapy room.

For example, Amy discloses to me, "I've been having an affair with a co-worker. My partner Allan suspects it's going on, but I've never admitted it to him."

My question to Amy is, "So how do you want to go about letting Allan know about the affair in our next couple's session? Would you like me to bring it up, or do you want to take the lead?"

If Amy is adamant about not telling Allan about her lover,

I will let both of them know I will not treat them. Honesty is the first step to repairing a damaged relationship. If either or both of the partners are not honest, I won't be able to do my job effectively.

When affairs are not disclosed in a couple's therapy, it causes problems. Several times I have suspected one of the partners of infidelity; stone-faced, they denied it to me and to their partner. This led me to believe that the individual must be suffering from some sort of clinical turmoil, such as a major depressive episode. It may appear that a patient is disconnected from her partner and from family members, showing little emotion. She has withdrawn from household responsibilities and has an irritable edge. She may also be blunting her emotional struggles with long hours at the office. And in therapy she seems so paralyzed, unwilling to take chances to change the sad state of her relationship. At first blush, it really seems that she's depressed. But no! Look again, Dr. Castro! She is having sex with a hot young attorney twice a week, and aside from feeling some guilt, my patient is feeling alive and well in her secret life.

Concerning Patrick and Susan's situation, no major issue like an affair existed. Their marital struggles simply underscored a vague unhappiness they both felt. While affirming that they wanted their marriage to get better, neither had any idea how to go about it. I prompted them, "Okay, guys, you are not sure about your goals in the couples therapy, or how to make things better. So let's start with this question: What do you guess is the one thing healthy couples frequently say when asked, *'What is the key to your happy relationship?'"*

Often couples will answer this question with "The partners share common interests" or "The partners share core beliefs on topics such as religion or family values." Sure, there certainly is a positive correlation between having a lot in common and having a successful relationship. In my experience, the saying "Birds of a feather flock together" is truer than "Opposites attract."

But the answer to this question, "What do healthy couples have in common?" is not about mutual interests. The answer comes down to one word. Healthy, satisfied couples describe their relationship as *"work"*! In so many ways, when you discuss what makes their successful marriage tick, both partners disclose that their relationship is always in the forefront of their minds and that they are constantly working on it. They will say, "I am always thinking about ways to improve my relationship with her" or "I focus on putting great effort into tending to his needs." These phrases, "ways to improve" and "putting great effort" use *active* words and speak to the lively engagement that goes into making a relationship healthy. Being in a healthy, intimate relationship is not a static state of being! It is not a given! It is about getting off your butt, taking the risk to get in the game, and Giving Room to working at it! Giving Room to work on your relationship is about fighting through the frustrating feelings that can arise during a heated discussion with your partner and stepping *forward* by expressing your thoughts and feelings in an honest and genuine way. Don't step backward and evade your emotions! Don't close down! Don't run away! Give Room by encouraging the dialog to continue. Create Space for your partner to also step forward and express his or her feelings.

"In order to have a strong relationship you need to work at it." It sounds so elementary, but this simple truth also illustrates another common feature of successful relationships.

That is, they are *fluid*. Like a mountain stream forging its path as it comes alive in springtime after the dead of winter, relationships also ebb and flow along constantly changing paths. What does the fluidity of your relationship have to do with your marriage? Answer: EVERYTHING! Your relationship is either getting better or it's getting worse! Relationships are not motionless.

So, there are two key elements to healthy relationships. First, they require work; second, they are fluid. Often, the intimate relationship that started off with such love and vigor (like Patrick and Susan's marriage) experiences an agonizingly slow death. I'm sure there are many reasons why the divorce rate in the United States is about 50 percent, but I strongly believe one reason is that couples do not understand that for their *marriage* to work, *they* need to work very hard.

Remember when I stressed that we all need to know we have someone who is in our corner? The simplest way to *work* on your intimate relationship is to constantly ask yourself the question "What can I do for my partner to make him or her feel I am in their corner?" I use the word *constantly* to emphasize that, like a flowing stream, the work of maintaining a healthy marriage never stops, and if we are not hypervigilant about regularly improving the relationship by tending to our partners, feelings will, sadly, shift for the worse.

Susan Johnson, a renowned couples therapist and theorist based in Ottawa, Canada, emphasizes the need, deep within the human soul, to have a partner who is in one's corner. Johnson's work, which derives from attachment theory, focuses on helping couples connect to the deep emotions that have been inspired by the individual's relationships throughout life. When one discusses attachment theory, early relationships in a person's life are naturally emphasized. I heard Johnson speak one time; she is brilliant. Hearing her talk about how she and her husband are in each other's corner made me think about my own marriage. She gave the example of being terrified of flying. What gets her through those long flights to the States to give professional talks is her husband's "voice" in her head saying, "Now, Sue, I am here with you. Nothing bad is going to happen. I am not going to allow anything bad to happen."

I don't know Sue Johnson personally, but I have to imagine that the strength of her marriage comes from her and her husband *actively working* at being in each other's corner. The fact that she can deal with her fear of flying by using messages about her husband being in her corner as she flies the scary skies speaks volumes about their commitment to work on the relationship.

I'm sure many of you feel determined to shift your intimate relationship to a more active and working relationship. You may be thinking, *Wow, my marriage is way down on my to-do list. In fact, Item 1 on today's list is "Meet Muriel S. for coffee at Starbucks." That's way ahead of "Work on marriage"!* I'll wager that many of you may not have "Work on Marriage" anywhere on your to-do list. You are not alone. Remember, too often we get caught up in the Rat Race, which makes life seem to pass by pretty quickly and causes us to pass over important issues. It is vital to hold "Work on Marriage" at the forefront of our minds and at the top of the to-do list.

Consistently pushing yourself to remain in your partner's corner is the first step along the road to a fulfilling, intimate relationship. But what happens if your partner isn't clear in communicating his or her needs? What will you do if making your partner feel "held" is constantly at the forefront of your mind, yet your partner doesn't show you how they want to be loved? Suppose you're motivated to Give Your Partner Room to Grow, and you are truly ready to take action, but your partner doesn't give you a sense of how to do it? What if there are no instructions? I will tell you exactly what happens: You will become frustrated and, more than likely, you will give up. The marriage will *fail*.

That is why, even before you and your partner can truly be in each other's corner, both of you need to get in touch with your most intimate needs and, in a clear and loving manner, communicate what those needs are. By reaching out to your partner and saying, "What I need from you is . . ." you are giving your partner a roadmap for the journey that is a fulfilling relationship for years to come. However, there is a slight problem when you express your needs so clearly. You are leaving yourself in a very vulnerable position. By asking your partner to be sensitive and responsive to your needs, you are certainly taking a big risk! Because once you pour out your heart in such an honest way to your partner, the experiment begins. You will now learn whether your partner is willing and/or able to care about you deeply.

It is very possible that your partner will embrace your courage by reaching out to you as well, in his or her own courageous way. With any luck, that one person whom you have chosen to walk with through life, hand in hand, will step up and answer your call. Your risk will have paid off: your partner will be committed to the work and the joy of being in your corner. Your transparency will have brought you two closer together.

Sadly, though, the opposite may happen. Having risked

putting all your cards on the table, you may be left disappointed. You ventured out, taking that scary step by opening up to your partner, yet, he or she may still not be there to catch you and make you feel loved and supported.

When the latter happens, feelings of sadness and frustration are especially strong. It's a very painful place to be. The moment it becomes evident that husband or wife cannot or will not Give Room to the needs of their partner, a palpable sadness fills the therapy room. The couple feels the sorrow, and so do I. Yet, ironically, whether the relationship is moving in a positive or negative direction, by expressing one's needs, *clarity* emerges. When both partners risk expressing their needs in a sincere manner, the landscape of the marriage becomes much more understandable and visible.

As a couples therapist, that is my number-one goal: to help clear the path (remember de-Velcroing the mind?) and provide clarity in the relationship. My primary job is helping the couple to see the relationship for what it truly is, then assisting them in taking positive steps away from the broken aspects of their relationship. It is not my job to tell a couple to get divorced, to separate, or to "stick it out for the long haul"! Who am I to make such an important, life-changing decision for someone else? The bottom line is that there is no set rule for how a couple should proceed in their relationship. Obviously, I am a big fan of marriage. Even though my wife has a unique talent for getting under my skin (and vice versa!), I am happily married and feel there is no better way to walk through life and experience all of its amazing moments than with a partner by my side. But I don't buy it when a couple says to me, "We have to stick with the marriage for the kids' sake." Research has shown that the absolute, number-one worst environment for children is one in which parents stay in the marriage and are constantly fighting and disrespectful to each other.

As a psychologist, I offer resources to help these individuals in pain to honestly assess their relationship. I encourage the couple to slow down and prioritize by Giving Room to the possibility that their marriage can once again be filled with intimacy and fun. We discuss the importance of taking a deep breath and Creating Space to look at their issues with a critical eye, de-Velcroing their separate expectations and assumptions about the relationship. In order to do this, the couple needs to slow down and step toward their struggles by Giving Room to assess their relationship. It is my job to help couples determine if they are willing to put in the work to change the current state of their relationship. It is such a critical and emotional moment when we arrive at that point. The couple doesn't even have to ask me, "What do we do now?" If they are doing the work, expressing their needs, and staying in each other's corner, they are energized and plow forward. Eventually, I just need to get out of the way and let them do their work! Yet, if the proverbial writing is on the wall and the relationship is completely motionless, the sadness of its demise fills my office.

Giving Room to taking risks and describing your needs in *any* intimate relationship is one of the master keys to a more meaningful life. Taking risks doesn't just have to be with your partner. When we take that scary step of describing our needs with complete honesty to all the important people in our lives, knowing we might get hurt, space for healthy growth is opened up in all relationships.

An incident with my father years ago clearly illustrates the power of what can happen when we take risks in relationships to honestly describe our needs. I took a risk with my father, putting myself in the vulnerable position that I just described. My dad is a no-nonsense type of guy. Frankly, it is impossible for him to hold back or sugarcoat his words when he has something on his mind, especially when it has to do with giving his kids advice. Sure, his words of guidance in my younger years served me well. Dad would instruct, "Son, it's a no-brainer that you should go to Penn State. It has the best reputation and the most opportunities." Or he would advise, "Playing many sports is a waste of time, son. Just stick with one and get really good at it." Or he would say confidently, "Yeah, I know, son. You're sad this person doesn't want to be your friend anymore, but trust me, rarely do you keep the same friends in life that you had as a kid. Let it go." Over and over, Dad's all-knowing pronouncements eased my intense feelings of worry, confusion, or sadness. It made traveling through childhood feel like I was on autopilot.

But once I moved out to Seattle for my postgraduate work and was under the care of my new male role model and supervisor, John Yurich, I really started to challenge my dad's opinions. Most of the time, my father's words of wisdom were right on the mark. My dad didn't know everything, but he was well read, street-smart, a hugely successful entrepreneur, and he had a ton of common sense. I couldn't argue with this track record. But now, in my young adult life, I was beginning to become more and more annoyed with my father feeling he had the right to lecture me on what direction my life should take.

It all came to a head when my parents came to visit my wife, Missy, and me in Seattle. We were eating dinner at a delightful restaurant perched atop a bluff just outside of downtown Seattle. It was a picturesque evening—the sun was actually shining! The four of us enjoyed a great meal and a few bottles of Chianti. The conversation began lightly as we first discussed my siblings and what was going on in their lives and then provided updates on Missy's parents and sister. Then the predictable shift happened in my father. "So, son, what do you guys plan to do in six months when the internship is over?"

In the past I would have answered my dad's question with a question: "Well, there are a lot of options, Dad. What do you think we should do?" But I was now at a point where my decisions would significantly affect my professional life, and therefore I wasn't interested in Dad's opinion. I had prepared for this question. I knew it would be coming sometime over the weekend and I had rehearsed what I wanted to say. Nevertheless, when the question came, Missy and I both squirmed in our chairs and our hearts began to race. I cleared my throat and began speaking the rehearsed words: "Well, as you know, Dad, in my profession and with my degrees, I can pretty much go anywhere in the country. So Missy and I have made the decision to settle in St. Louis and begin raising a family."

Dad seemed prepared for my answer and immediately went into a litany of reasons why it would be a huge mistake to move to Missy's hometown of St. Louis and not return to the DC area. I didn't flinch. I stayed calm, smiled, and nodded. Again, my dad knows a lot about many things, but I actually knew more than he did when it came to job opportunities in my field as a practicing psychologist. Have you ever experienced a moment like this in your own life when you knew exactly the path you wanted to take? You were certain of it—so certain that you could duel confidently with your old man!

In a respectful manner, I countered his argument for over thirty minutes, sticking to the facts. I had earned three degrees, I had a postdoctoral internship under my belt, we had the support of Missy's family, and so on. I had done my homework and although I didn't have a job lined up yet, I was optimistic about the opportunities in St. Louis. And then, for the first time in my life, my dad infuriated me. He realized I wasn't budging on my position. It was a done deal—Missy and I were moving to the Midwest. He finally lost all composure and in a loud, angry voice, he bellowed, "The only reason you're moving to St. Louis is because Missy wants to be near her family and she's obviously controlling you!"

Mind you, Missy was sitting right next to me when my dad made this rude and cutting remark. Furthermore, his comment was so far from the truth! I love my wife, but anyone who knows Missy clearly understands she is the opposite of "the controlling wife." In fact, too often I feel she lets others take advantage of her. At that moment, when he said those words, I had had enough. I stood up, threw my napkin down, and pointed at him. "This conversation is over!" Then I stormed off to the bathroom. The rest of the weekend was fine, yet there was obviously tension in the air. My parents knew I wasn't happy with them and they were smart not to bring up the topic again. I took the risk of expressing my feelings to my father, and I was clearly vulnerable. So were they.

The story is not over, though. Fast-forward six months, the next time I was with my father. My internship was complete, and my now-pregnant wife had already moved into our new home in St. Louis. My car was packed, and I was ready for the two-day drive to start my new life and new job in the Show Me State. Surprisingly, I got a call from my father a week before I was scheduled to depart Seattle. Dad insisted that he fly into Seattle and join me on the long drive. He casually said, "I've never seen that part of the country, plus it will be nice for us to spend some time together." Thanks to the "Slugfest in Seattle," I wasn't nervous about talking to my father about anything, so the thought of spending that much time alone with him seemed kind of nice.

At some point during the second day of our drive (I believe somewhere in the Dakotas), I had the urge to really open up to my father about something very important to me that I had been thinking about. I wanted to disclose something I felt I really needed from him. (Note that this situation is *no different* than that of a healthy marriage. I was taking a risk and expressing my needs in a relationship that was important to me.) Driving along, we hadn't spoken for a good hour when I broke the silence. I said, "Dad, I want to talk to you about something important."

Dad straightened up in the passenger seat. "What is it, son?"

I took the risk. "Well, all my life you have been a great dad and you have given some great advice over the years, not to mention all the material things you have provided me with. But at this point in my life, I need to ask you for something. What I need is: If I don't ask for your advice, I don't want it. If I want some advice from you, I will absolutely ask, because you definitely have a lot to offer. But if I don't ask you for advice on any topic that has to do with my life, it means I don't want it."

There. I did it. I finally let him have it, sharing with my father my most basic *need* at that time in my life: the need for independence. I needed to let my dad know that while I appreciated and respected his free advice, I no longer wanted it to come unsolicited. My dad didn't respond immediately. He sat with my words for a good minute or two.

Then he said, sternly, "Anthony, I cannot do that for you. I feel as your father that if there is advice that I want to give you and that I feel you need to hear, I am going to say it, no matter what. I'm sorry I can't give you what you want, and I know you might be upset to hear it. But I would rather die knowing I did everything that I feel defines a good father—like giving advice, even if you don't like me for it—than to keep my mouth shut and make you happy by giving you what you want."

I asked, "Dad, even if I end up resenting and hating you for it, you will still give advice?"

Shaking his head. "Yes."

I sat in silence for a good minute or two and then said, "Okay."

It was a moment that shifted our father-son relationship. When he spoke his words and very directly told me that he wouldn't be able to give me what I wanted, I was filled with sadness. I was sad to feel that my father couldn't give me what I needed. Yet, ironically, along with feeling sad, I also felt closer to my father. He was so honest with his words. Even though we didn't agree, we were engaged in an intimate, emotion-filled dialogue. As the years have passed, I look back on that conversation as a moment that brought us closer together. Sure, my father continues to give advice, and it definitely annoys me at times. But now his words of advice also communicate to me that he takes his job as a father very seriously and wants to do his best. Plus, I can't help but listen to his valuable insights from time to time.

I described this situation with my father to show that in any relationship, whether inside or outside of your family, expressing your needs Gives Room for growth and intimacy. We must Create the Space to be vulnerable and describe our needs to the people most important in our lives. I didn't get what I wanted and needed from my father, just like we will never get everything we want and need from our partners, no matter how honestly and clearly we ask for it. But by Giving Room and space to sincerely describe our feelings, intimacy emerges. By taking the risk and putting ourselves in a vulnerable position, clarity surfaces about the importance of relationships. This is Giving Room: Taking risks and opening up your feelings and needs to others. Also, it is important to note that when a couple describes needs, and both individuals are on different pages (as with my father and me), the fact that both have taken a chance and opened up makes it easier to move from one's own stance, even if it is a very small move. By Creating the Space and Giving Room, change is certain to occur. As I mentioned, my father continues to give advice, but I sense, at times, that he holds back his words of wisdom because he knows that's what I want.

I have spent some time discussing the importance of letting others know your needs. Giving Room to express our needs helps us see the level of intimacy in the relationship, whether with your partner, with a parent, or in another significant relationship. Now, let me give you a specific way to buckle down and work on your intimate relationships.

A helpful way to continually work on improving a relationship is to schedule time for it. Couples will complain, "Dr. Castro, setting an appointment to work on the relationship doesn't seem especially romantic or authentic. Shouldn't doing things for or with my partner be more real, more spontaneous, and coming from the heart?"

Sure, surprising your spouse with flowers on any old Tuesday ("just because") is a lovely and loving gesture. But to build an incredibly strong fortress of a marriage, you need to start with the basic steel beams that represent the foundation of any stable relationship. By scheduling a time to improve the marriage, just like scheduling a time to meet your best friend at Starbucks, you have laid the groundwork for a solid marriage.

This was the problem for Patrick and Susan. Patrick was putting in fifty-plus hours at work, and Susan was working four twelve-hour shifts in the operating room and picking up overtime along the way. Their minds were never focused on the marriage because too much other "stuff" was flooding them. It was time to build a dam to halt the rushing Rat Race flood that had swept them away from their relationship. I proposed, "Okay, we need a time during the week when you two can talk alone with no distractions. Certainly our therapy is one forum for this type of interaction, but I also need you two to take a risk by Giving Room to extend it beyond the therapy hour. So what do you think?" Patrick and Susan needed to be nudged to Create Space for prioritizing their relationship. They had to Give Room to focusing on the marriage, not just work. Why? Because that is what they wanted. They desperately wanted to reconnect with each other. It was time to Give Room.

Patrick and Susan had made great progress in therapy. They were able to get in touch with their scary and vulnerable feelings and express them in a nonthreatening way to each other. Improving their intimate communication was quite difficult in the beginning. As I discussed in chapter 2, in the section "The Script," at times I needed to help Patrick and Susan by providing them with the words. Giving a client a script is very similar to a technique developed by Dan Wile, a well-known couples therapist and writer in San Francisco. Dr. Wile will actually scoot his rolling chair back and forth and talk as if he were the partner. "Okay, Patrick, I want to make sure Susan understands what you are trying to say so I am going to pretend to be you, and you let me know what part is right and what part is wrong." Using a script, Wile's technique, and other methods—along with the courage of Patrick and Susan—therapy wasn't exactly fun, but it was paying off.

But when I asked them to take it to the next level and partake in weekly therapy sessions alone, they fought the idea. Patrick said, "Nah, I don't think that is going to work, Dr. C. Our schedules are just crazy and they don't match up well enough." Susan was more honest. "We probably could find a time to do it, but I'm a little nervous about it. I'm afraid we won't make it a priority and would just blow it off. Then we would be back to square one."

During the next few sessions, Patrick and Susan focused on reassuring each other that they had been, and continue to be, committed to their relationship. Their communication skills had immensely improved. They had grown as a couple and didn't need to be so dependent on me. Just like kids starting to get the hang of riding a bike, Patrick and Susan just needed a push and then for me to let go. Susan took the first scary step. "You know, Patrick, on Wednesdays you always seem to have downtime at work from 2:00 to 3:30. You could come home and we could talk for forty-five minutes and then get a late lunch."

Uneasy, Patrick pushed himself and agreed. "Yeah, that actually would work. Let's give it a try."

Patrick and Susan continue to see me, but now the couple's sessions are six to eight weeks apart rather than weekly. They have graduated to "maintenance therapy," which is essentially a checkup to make sure things are on track. I also request that they come back at least every few months so that I can see the pictures of their two darling girls. Currently, they rank their marriage at an eight. I recently asked them, "Okay, guys, what do you need to do to keep that number high or to get the number even higher?" They laughed, "Yeah, yeah, we know! Just keep working on it!" Susan and Patrick know I will always be as relentless as a drill sergeant, pushing them to put in the time and work to make their marriage a priority. With a grin, I tell them, "If you truly feel you have put your marriage at the top of your to-do list *daily*, I have no problem with you meeting your old friend for coffee at that great American establishment, Starbucks!"

Giving Room for healthy growth in your intimate relationship takes time and work and it requires taking chances. As life whizzes by, we tend to lose precious opportunities to slow down and look deep into our partner's eyes. Taking the time to "connect with our eyes" is one of the most intimate forms of communication you can experience with your loved one. It brings understanding and compassion. So make it a priority to look into your partner's eyes more often! Responding to a loved one's needs, or at least honestly letting that person know you are not willing or able to meet certain needs, Gives Room for growth. And finally, it is vital to see your marriage as being at the pinnacle of your own personal "hierarchy of life." Every other priority—your job, your hobbies, your pets, your vacations, volunteer work, and yes, even your kids—should all trickle down from there. Your marriage needs to be at the top of your daily to-do list!

GIVING ROOM TO A "CARING EAR"

From time to time, I am asked to respond to an "Open Mind" question. "Open Mind" is a weekly column that appears in several Missouri newspapers. Readers send in questions regarding mental health issues, and these questions are answered by professional contributors. Below are two questions posed to me by "Open Mind" readers, followed by my responses. While reading my two answers, I want you to think about how my responses are similar in both of these very different issues presented.

Sixteen-Year-Old Is Afraid of Darkness

Dear Open Mind: I recently married a very nice man, a widower, with two adolescent children. His daughter is sixteen; his son is twelve. They seem to be happy, well-adjusted children with one exception. The daughter is afraid of the dark. Her bedroom light must be left on, as well as the light outside her door in the hallway. This has been going on for about three years. Her fear of darkness doesn't seem to be related to the loss of her mother, which occurred about five years ago. How do you think I can help her?

My Response: Sadness, anger, resentment, relief, guilt, fear. Similar to divorce, the death of a parent digs astonishingly deep into a child's memory bank. Although children are quite resilient and can bury intense emotions, these feelings are often expressed through behaviors that negatively affect development.

It makes sense that the symptoms (fear of darkness) emerged two years after the mother's death. The emotional development of a girl as she transitions into a young woman can be unsettling and confusing. The struggle with "finding one's individuality" and "fearing the unknown" pulls the adolescent to behave (or misbehave) in many ways. For some teenagers the transition is smooth; others plunge into this challenge in a rebellious manner. Yet others will shy away from the darkness and mysteries of their future, particularly a child who lost her mother at the age of eleven.

Giving the child room, access, and encouragement to discuss this struggle is the key. She may be comfortable talking to you, her dad, a friend, a neighbor, the school counselor, or her grandma. Whoever the person is should listen and support her in an empathetic and caring way but should not shy away from the difficult feelings.

Fourteen-Year-Old Daughter Was Arrested for Shoplifting

Dear Open Mind: Recently my wife and I were shocked to learn that our fourteen-year-old daughter was arrested for shoplifting. Until then, her rebelliousness was fairly typical of an adolescent making the transition from child to adult. But we're really concerned now since her behavior has moved in the direction of breaking the law. What makes a child steal when they have money to pay for things? How can we know if this is the beginning of a pattern?

My Response: One "Psycho-Babble" phrase for such a behavior is "Acting Out," which describes the external behavioral expression of what is an internal emotional struggle. Possibly, through her behavior your child is crying out, "Look at me! I need some help!" Teenagers often face challenges that feel overwhelming—like failures in their efforts to perform academically, socially, or on the athletic field. There's also the fear of being shunned by friends, peer pressure concerning drugs and alcohol, developing one's individuality, and let us not forget the Mother of All Teenage Neuroses, getting your heart broken! Your daughter is likely acting out because something hurts inside. As parents, our lives are so busy that it is difficult to spend the needed time to really listen when our kids are speaking. But we must, if we truly want them to flourish in life. Just listening without giving advice may feel like you are shirking your parental responsibility for setting limits, but it is in fact an excellent opportunity to communicate to your daughter that you are in her corner and you are ready to listen. It is the pattern of "all work and very little family time" so common in our society that needs to be of concern. If you invest the time and do this for your kids, the returns will be immeasurable.

In addition to my response, another professional answered each question. Concerning the sixteen-year-old who was afraid of the dark, the other psychologist's response focused on "solving the problem." His answer mapped out behavioral ways to tackle this one symptom (keeping the light on when falling asleep), such as implementing relaxation techniques right before bedtime. He also talked about combating the symptom by taking it in stages, such as decreasing the illumination of the light little by little (*systematic desensitization* is the term for this behavioral technique). The focus of his treatment came from the belief that if the primary symptom goes away, "all is good!" and the child will sleep soundly in the dark.

A professional from Family Court responded to the question about the light-fingered fourteen-year-old. Similar to the response above that focused on eliminating the symptom, this professional went into detail about the array of state-funded programs that educate and discipline young offenders for breaking the law. Furthermore, she cited the low percentage of repeat offenders among those who go through the court's rehabilitation process.

Focusing on symptom relief is not a bad thing, and I fully support educational programs paid for by the state, through our tax money, to help young offenders turn their lives around. Also, teaching patients relaxation techniques and leading clients through a systematic desensitization program (particularly if they are dealing with a phobia) is common practice in my office. In general, behavioral techniques can be quite helpful. Furthermore, sometimes patients will demand a direct and symptom-focused approach. Within the first five minutes of meeting me, the individual may say, "Let me tell you exactly what I want. I am hiring you as my therapist to give me specific techniques to combat this issue." If I feel the individual needs "something else" in therapy, I will tell him. But I always let my patients know that they are the boss, and if behavioral techniques are what they want, I certainly have a bagful of them.

But to me, the two questions posed by these concerned parents had more to do with a "young voice not being heard" than with specific problems needing to be fixed. The symptoms, breaking the law and being afraid of the dark, were the results of a need not being met and an emotional strain not being talked about. To both queries, I offered some explanations as to why these teens might be struggling internally. For the girl who sleeps with the lights on, her inner turmoil likely has to do with the loss of her mother and the difficult transitions into womanhood. For the young one who is stealing, her internal difficulties likely stem from peer pressure or dealing with "not fitting in." Truthfully, there are no "quick fixes" for these broad life events that have given birth to the unwanted behaviors. As the saying goes, "It is what it is!" A mother has died, and she can no longer comfort and support her adolescent daughter as she makes the scary passage into young adulthood. There is no stopping the devastating feelings of a young one who loses a parent. No behavioral technique can make everything all better. Furthermore, the waves of insecurity and anxiety that crash down on a teenager who's trying to fit in with peers aren't going to immediately subside or vanish with communication or socialization training. Targeting the symptoms of these two kids serves only as a bandage that will eventually fall off, leaving the emotional wounds exposed and at risk of infection.

Giving Room for people to vent their feelings is so simple yet vitally important in the development of healthy relationships. Unfortunately, many of us are caught up in mindless sprints through the mazes and over the hurdles of the Rat Race. If a problem occurs, we quickly exit the race, work to fix the problem with intense speed, and then jump right back in! Spending the time to Give Room and sit with the feelings without the urge to find an immediate fix is a tremendous gift you give to yourself. Just like the parents who wrote to the "Open Mind" column, I see parents demanding me to give them ways to "fix" their kids. They will plead, "Little Suzie has been so defiant since her baby triplet sisters were born. She is hell on wheels! How can we fix her bad behavior?"

Perhaps the answer is "Maybe it isn't the child that needs fixing?!" In her outstanding book *The Blessing of a Skinned Knee*, Dr. Wendy Mogel, a clinical child psychologist, drives home the point that we as parents often portray our kids as psychologically unstable and feel the pressure to fix them, yet maybe it isn't the child who has the issue. She talks about how, early in her career, parents brought their kids to her office for psychological evaluation. One would expect these parents to breathe a sigh of relief when Dr. Mogel reviewed the healthy test results, indicating that their child was psychologically and intellectually "good enough"—results that showed no major emotional or cognitive deficits. Oddly, though, most of these parents were disappointed when hearing the good news. They wished there was a specific problem with a well-defined solution that would fix it!

As a young professional, I fell into the trap of regarding therapy as a place to fix my patients' tangible issues, as opposed to being a place that Gives Them Room for emotional expression. I experienced this misunderstanding at the American University Counseling Center, where I worked as a therapist during one of my early externship-training years. By the end of the second week at American University, I was terribly discouraged about my ability to help these students. Over and over, students would come to my office and emotionally throw up! Within a minute of the session beginning, tears would be flowing as these rattled kids spewed all their college-life stresses. By this time in my training, I was well versed in "Empathic Reflection 101." My ability to sit with the student and take in, understand, and reflect back his or her array of feelings was pretty good. Typically, by the end of an initial session, the tissue box would be empty and it was pretty evident the student felt relief. We would end by pulling out our scheduling books and setting up our next session for the following week.

The problem was, more times than not, my clients never returned for their second appointment! I was devastated! What had gone wrong? How did I screw up? Did I talk too much? Did I not say enough? Maybe they could tell I was nervous and green? I finally got up enough nerve and, with my tail between my legs, I broached the topic with my supervisor. I explained, "I don't understand it. I can't say I'm the best therapist around, but at least I know that these students who never returned felt comfortable with me and that they felt heard when we were together. Why aren't they returning?"

Surprisingly, my supervisor nodded and smiled with reassurance. "I'm sure you were very attentive to their emotional needs, Anthony. I bet you were right with those kids the entire session. Yes, you did your job."

Confused, I asked, "But why didn't they come back? How did I scare them off?"

Her response was instrumental in my development as a clinician for years to come. She said, "The reason they didn't come back is because they got what they needed."

Such an important lesson! It has stuck with me throughout my career. My supervisor was right. Many of those students just needed a "caring ear" to listen to and accept what they had to say. They needed someone to Give Room to just listen, someone they could really feel was in their corner. No advice needed to be given. No problem solving needed to be done. And no course of long-term treatment needed to be utilized. These emotionally overwhelmed students just needed a safe and accepting harbor where they could express themselves in a very honest way.

Parents sometimes struggle with this concept when I describe it to them; it is hard for these caregivers to understand. As I said in one of my "Open Mind" responses, "Just listening without giving advice may feel like you are shirking your parental responsibility for setting limits, but it is in fact an excellent opportunity to communicate to your daughter that you are in her corner and you are ready to listen."

Parents react to this kind of advice with frustration. "I just don't know how to do it—how to, as you say, give my kid a 'caring ear.'"

I will coach these parents, "Just do what we silly therapists do all the time. Just repeat what your kid says. Just say what they say." I often give an example: "Okay, so little Jaeden comes home from school and starts talking about his sad and frustrating feelings. He explains how he wanted to play kickball with the other kids during recess but that his peers shunned him." I then say to Mom, "Okay, now you be Jaeden, and I will be you."

Mom pretends to be Jaeden, doing her best to describe the unfortunate situation. "Mom, I was really sad when I asked if I could play and they ignored me."

I jump in as Mom. "Wow, Jaeden. I bet that made you feel really sad and frustrated when they didn't even answer your question."

"You bet it did," fires back Mom.

"And it sounds like you were so frustrated and upset with the situation that you didn't even know what to do."

Mom bellows, "That's right! I felt so stuck!"

By simply reflecting her child's hurt feelings, Mom has reinforced her son's hurt feelings and comforted him. You don't have to be a clinical psychologist to develop the skill of well-timed reflections. Empathic reflections are a great way for parents to attend to their child's feelings. It is the emotional pull to "fix it" that throws parents off. As you know, I'm a parent too. I can easily imagine if Jaeden were my Zoe, I would be furious! I'd definitely want to *fix* the issue right away!

The rule I set for parents is: "If you feel compelled to advise your kid on how to address or fix a problem in his or her life, you must first ask them for 'permission.'" For example, Mom may want to explain to Jaeden how to assertively, yet respectfully, insert himself in the kickball game. I tell Mom that she can give her advice only if she asks and receives her son's permission to express her words of wisdom. However, even if Jaeden says it's okay for Mom to give her input, the empathic reflections of her caring ear still need to precede the advice. For example: "You know, Jaeden, for the past thirty minutes you've been talking about that sad and frustrating situation you ran into during recess. And I think I really understand how upset and stuck you must have felt. But I was thinking that there might be a way to address the situation at recess if it ever happens again. So I was wondering if you wanted to hear my advice on how to maybe fix this issue?"

If Jaeden shakes his head *no* and says, "That's okay, Mom," you are not allowed to say any more about the solution! Jaeden didn't give you permission! However, if he gives you a curious look and says, "Okay, what do you think?" feel free to open the floodgates to your teaching, guiding, explaining, coaching, mentoring, and so on. But don't let it drag on too long or you will lose your child's attention. (I call this the "Thirty Seconds Rule." You will lose your kid's interest after thirty seconds of lecturing.) Your child might shut you down and refuse to give you permission to give advice because what's usually needed has nothing to do with advice! It has to do with being "heard." We often underestimate our kids' intelligence. It's likely that Jaeden has already considered some possible "solutions." Furthermore, there is a good chance that he has already implemented the solutions and somewhat rectified the situation. What he really needs is a safe place to air his feelings.

The point is, Giving Room with a caring ear and allowing others to describe and elaborate their most intimate and vulnerable feelings is a precious gift for both parties. Giving

Room and allowing others to vent helps strengthen any kind of relationship and is indispensable to intimacy.

Let me conclude with what might seem like a silly thought. When it comes to this issue of lending others a caring ear, we might take a lesson from our furry four-legged friends. That's right, dogs are the most unbelievable experts at "just listening" and letting you know "I am here for you; feel free to dump it all out!" Thank goodness dogs don't speak! By not having a more highly evolved brain and vocal cords, dogs don't have the opportunity to screw up and bog down an emotionally filled moment with words! As a matter of fact, you can't go wrong adding dogs to your list of empathetic friends when you need to let your emotions out. I've seen it time and time again with both adults and kids. Nothing is more therapeutic and comforting for children when they are crying in bed about something very sad (such as just learning their parents are divorcing) than to have their dog snuggling up to them. As tears soak the pup's coat, both slowly drift off into a cloudless sleep. Now that's Giving Room.

Conclusion

HOLLY AND GIVING ROOM

HOLLY'S TOUGH ROAD AHEAD

So what do you think is in store for Holly as she and her sister are greeted by their mother at the bus station after their fun-filled summer on the farm with Grandpa? Holly's eleventh birthday is right around the corner, and she begins the sixth grade in two weeks. What road will Holly travel? What path will this preteen take? How will life change or how will it stay the same over the next week? Month? Year? Five years? There is no doubt that the first ten years of this little girl's life have been deprived of a "good-enough" mother. How will this lack of a *consistent*, loving caregiver impact the rest of Holly's life?

The good news is that kids are resilient and can frequently bounce back from difficult, even traumatic events in their childhood. This might be the case even for Holly and her sister. I see it every day in my practice. Several years ago I treated a little girl named Bella, who witnessed her father violently beat and burn his stepson to death. Bella's mother was serving time for drug dealing. From age four to seven, Bella's life was chaotic and constantly changing. Her father never lashed out at her physically, but he abused her emotionally by belittling her and telling her she was worthless.

After the fatal beating occurred, Bella was court-ordered to live with her aunt and uncle and their four kids. For two years, I treated Bella at weekly sessions. In the beginning, she experienced occasional nightmares about the horrific scene. Also, her demeanor was one of shyness in the home, at her new school, and in my office. Yet within months, Bella came out of her shell and began reaching out to others. She made friends quickly, participated in extracurricular activities such as dance and piano, and her grades were above average. She rarely talked about her stepbrother's death or about the imprisonment of her father and mother. Bella was focused on her new life and she embraced it. I would do the "therapy dance" around the horrible topic, and Bella would reciprocate, usually through the therapeutic tool of play therapy. Sure, she would engage, when I pushed, about her troubled life. But many sessions were filled with what therapists call "surface material." Bella would not dive into the emotional pool of pain and deprivation she'd experienced while living with her parents. She stayed in the present, and the topics remained light. I did not become frustrated with these surface sessions. She would leave our sessions appearing to be emotionally stable, and her current life outside of therapy communicated to me that, "Yes, Bella is doing well!"

But then the unexpected happened in our second year of working together. As we were taking a walk over to the hospital attached to my office building to look at the newborn babies, Bella said to me, "You know, Dr. C, I was thinking about my father and how he was really mad at Jose, and how he was hurting him. I thought maybe I should talk to you about it because you're the person I'm supposed to talk about my feelings with." As she began to speak, amazingly, her words were matter-of-fact and her demeanor really didn't change. But ten minutes into our talk, as we approached the glass window where the newborns lay swaddled and asleep, fear and sadness started to take over Bella's face. She turned away from the babies and looked at me with her big, sad, dark eyes. "I didn't know what to do. Jose just kept crying and crying, and my daddy kept getting more and more angry."

As the session ended, I signaled to Bella's aunt with my hand up to my ear as if on a phone: *We need to talk.* Later that evening I explained to the aunt that the "floodgates had opened." We talked about how Bella's mind had decided to revisit the trauma and that her behavior might turn unpredictable over the next few weeks. I explained, "The deep stuff has now begun to surface, and Bella has given words to it. Get ready—she may struggle on many levels for a while." This warning to Bella's aunt demonstrates the natural flow of therapy. When we talk about tough stuff during therapy, we don't always feel good in the beginning, and in fact we may regress. But in the end, a sense of lightness will more often than not emerge. That is when we Give Room for growth.

Well, guess what happened over the next several weeks? To my surprise and delight, nothing really changed. Bella strolled into my office the following week with a big smile on her face, ready to talk to me about her goldfish and the fun she had with the neighborhood boy jumping on his trampoline. As I'm sure you guessed, I did bring up our discussion from a week earlier, but Bella really wasn't interested in talking more about it. She just kept smiling and focusing on what fun it is to "do a flip and land on your stomach!"

During the several months that followed "the session," Bella continued to thrive. Occasionally she would bring up the topic of her parents and the chaos she lived in during her younger years. But Bella wasn't very emotional during these discussions. She described the sad feelings, but she didn't seem very sad herself. She talked about her nervousness, but she didn't seem anxious. Week after week, Bella presented to me as being in the "good-enough" range for a kid her age. Furthermore, communication from the school and input from her aunt also told me, "Bella is doing well. She is emotionally stable." I was happy to learn that Bella's anxious and sad feelings were no different from those of any typical kid moving through the stresses of childhood, and that acting-out behavior, often seen as a disguise in emotionally troubled kids, just wasn't present. Over the past two years, Bella has come to see me every few months for a "check in." Occasionally, she will talk about some issues with friends or school, but for the most part, Bella continues to be a psychologically healthy child.

I share Bella's story to reiterate the resilient nature of kids. Like Bella's, Holly's psychological makeup acts like a pliable plastic trash bag being pushed and poked to its limit by an overabundance of junk. But it never tears. The psychological stress Holly experienced at the hands of her troubled mother clearly impacted her life, leaving deep scars, but her powerful mind helps hold her world in place and allows her to venture forward in life. Moreover, since Holly's mother has begun to accept the fact that she has an illness and needs to be in treatment (both psychotherapy and medication management), the odds of Holly being successful and happy in life will increase. In sum, Bella's story speaks to the fact that if kids are put in a good-enough environment—despite some rough times, as in Holly's case—they are likely to thrive. Kids are strong.

Yes, kids often bounce back from traumatic situations, but life events do impact us all. You can't get away from this truth in life—our environment plays a vital part in shaping who we are. Even though Holly is still a young child, eleven years is eleven years! Eleven years is a long time. I've been married a little over eleven years and let me tell you, it sometimes feels like an eternity! It's clear to see after reading about young Holly that changing the core of her personality is likely to be very difficult. As we have stressed before, people just don't like to change, and the nature of change goes against human nature. People get set in their ways, and it is so difficult to assist them in heading down a different, healthier path. Once we are running our own personal Rat Race, conditioned to any kind of maze or wheel, it is not easy to jump out.

This is true of Holly as well. Holly is clearly set in her ways, and for good reason. The rigid character traits she exhibits have been her adaptive survival tools. For example, Holly needed to be "on the clock" when orchestrating the morning and evening routines for herself and her sister. If not, disaster would strike. The fact was, just one misstep, and she and Katie would suffer.

She methodically begins pouring the coffee grounds into the coffee machine filter, then adds the water and presses the start button.

229

Mother's coffee will be ready in no time. Next, she pops a few slices of bread into the toaster oven for herself and her sister, Katie. A sliced bagel is tossed in for her mother. Her cat, Sunny, is next. She cleans out the litter box, refills her food bowl, and gives her fresh water.

Holly's to-do list is an example of her constantly using time to her advantage, helping to assuage the fear she must continually feel that things may not go as planned. Her rigid and regimented way of moving through her day helps her gain a sense of control in a world in which unpredictable events have been relentlessly thrown at her. Holly's uneasiness keeps her hyperfocused, and it stems from the reality that whenever she turns a corner, a curve ball may be racing toward her head! She needs to take control and be as prepared as possible simply in order to make it through childhood. Holly knows that with just one "false move," she is likely to be knocked down. And one day, the blow might just be too great, and she would be unable to get up.

Holly's *fear* of the world crumbling around her has certainly been a major impetus to "doing things the right way." In her mind, there is no room for error, no room for second best, no room for just "giving it your best shot." For this little girl, there just isn't any room for *Giving Room*. For to enter that great spaciousness in which one has been Given Room or is Giving Room—room in which to grow or simply to be—is just too great a risk for her.

Yet it is not only fear of destruction that pushes little Holly to always be on high alert. *Guilt* is also a driving force in her mind. As we discussed earlier, guilt is a nasty, paralyzing neurosis that bleeds through the vulnerable individual, contaminating everything. Nobody is perfect in their conduct, and at times it is appropriate to feel bad about our poor choices and inappropriate behavior. We all mess up, and it is certainly appropriate to feel bad when we do. But Holly's harsh feelings toward herself are downright irrational. When Holly's arm was broken—by her mother!—the fury and self-loathing she exhibited was completely inappropriate and devastating. Holly actually felt guilty for "allowing" such a thing to happen, because she knew there would be difficult consequences. Holly's guilt is also evident on the one day she forgets to put the front-door key in her backpack. Holly is furious at herself, scolding, *"Damn you, Holly! Damn you!"*

Holly's intense and irrational guilt is fueled by two sources. First, as I pointed out, there is no room for her to be just "good enough." In her mind, she needs to be perfect. Obviously, seeing life in such a black-and-white manner sets Holly up for disappointment in herself, no matter how smart or motivated she is. Sure, Holly's intense focus propels her to realize great-ness in life, but this same focus results in her being too hard on herself. Holly feels she must "get everything right" and she certainly comes close in many areas. But when it comes to living life, 100 percent mindfulness is not possible—or recom-mended—for anyone, even Holly. She struggles with Giving Room to being *good enough* (which she clearly is) in order to avoid her mother's wrath, but she feels she doesn't live up to her definition of "good enough," and so a shroud of guilt weighs heavily on her, never leaving her shoulders.

The second source of Holly's oppressive guilt comes from her mother. The reason Holly always has a critical eye focused on everything she does is because her unstable mother has reinforced that habit. We saw this unspeakable cruelty when Katie said that Holly "wasn't cleaning her right."

CONCLUSION

The look of pure evil and rage that shot from Mother's eyes as she entered the bathroom, leather belt in hand, is the look that neither Katie nor Holly will ever forget. The beating was brutal that night, leaving both girls with bright red welts up down their backs and bottoms. But it was the eyes—the savage eyes of a crazed animal—that produced the most painful blows, leaving deep scars in the girls' little brains.

The anger in their mother's eyes communicated not only rage but also conveyed to Holly: "You messed up and now you and your sister are going to pay!" Holly feels frightful bewilderment that she is doing everything she needs to do, but, being human, she inevitably missteps and "causes" her mother to punish her and her sister. Her critical mind screams again and again, *"Damn you, Holly! Damn you!"* The guilt is enormous.

Because she is constantly in a methodical survival mode born of fear and guilt, Holly is unable to slow down her life. She must always be "on." The responsibility that has been thrust upon Holly, both in reality and in her mind, leaves little room for this young child to Give Room to being a child. In almost every way, Holly has been robbed of her childhood and was forced to jump on the "Rat Race Train" way too early in life. A college graduate majoring in biology that just received her acceptance letter to medical school boards the Rat Race Train that will speed through her medical training over the next eight to ten years. But that young coed is twenty-two years old! Holly was only five when she began her research on becoming a doctor, leaving little room for Barbie dolls, play-dates with friends, and wishing upon a star.

Back to our original question: *What does life have in store for Holly as she celebrates her eleventh birthday?* One thing is for certain: Holly's chaotic, traumatic childhood has chiseled one message into her psyche, and that is that the world is pre-dictably unpredictable! The only thing predictable about Holly's life is—it is unpredictable!

Along with the ever-changing nature of Holly's world, this poor child has also been deprived of that consistent, loving mentor that every child needs. If anyone desperately needed someone in his or her corner, it's Holly. Sure, a few strong, pos-itive figures have played a role in Holly's young life, people like Emily's mother (Mrs. Peterson), Nurse Parker, and Grandpa. But Holly has lacked *consistent* empathy and *ongoing* support from an all-important and desperately needed caregiver.

To summarize, because of the unpredictable chaos of Holly's life, periodically detonated by her unstable mother, Holly is motivated by fear and guilt. And without that impor-tant, consistent caregiver in her corner offering stability and empathy, Holly has developed a hypercritical outlook on life and especially on herself. Her rigid attention to day-to-day tasks has deprived her of a childhood and earned her a one-way ticket on the Rat Race Express. *How does a childhood almost devoid of empathy and filled with inconsistency, instability, constant feelings of guilt and fear, and a harsh critical view of the world and of self, impact a soon-to-be eleven-year-old?*

The answer is: relational devastation.

Holly's most devastating loss is her inability to *trust* and to enjoy *intimacy*. Her challenge—both in years to come and today, as she blows out her imaginary candles on her imagi-nary cake, at her imaginary birthday party, with her sister and their stuffed animals circled around to celebrate—will be to open her arms and heart in *trust* and to Give Room for *inti-macy*. It goes almost without saying that in order to be truly intimate with another person—and with oneself—there needs

233

to be a solid foundation of trust in the relationship. How could Holly give herself to another person, or to herself, when bitter experience has taught her that nothing and no one can be counted on? In other words, Holly's relational foundation, produced by unreliable past relationships, will be on extremely shaky ground.

Will Holly Give Room to fight the guilt? Will she raise her arms in fierce independence to hold back the fast-moving Rat Race? Will she use her memory and lessons learned in childhood to beat the odds and live a fulfilling life? Will she Give Room for happiness at age eleven and beyond? Holly has a tough road ahead, but I am optimistic that she will. Let's review the steps that Holly—and all of us—must take in order to Give Room for a meaningful life.

EGO STRENGTH

The bold step to doing something different, the decision to endure change, the courage to venture forward and Give Yourself Room to enter into the unknown is the secret to a happier and more fulfilling life.

Different. Change. Unknown. These key words that make up the spirit of my message convey the following basic principle: If you don't Give Room to doing things differently in life, you will continue to feel the way you do. In other words: If you feel stuck and you want to change the way you feel and develop a deeper internal sense of purpose in life, you will need to move in a different direction. This is the action-oriented imperative for a rewarding life. Giving Room is not about "staying put" in our actions and mindset. *Actively* doing something different is the first and most needed step to changing your situation. However, while we do Give Room by taking action with something, we must sometimes do the opposite and "sit with it." I will describe this in a few paragraphs.

This is not to suggest that actively doing something different always means getting off your butt and intensely working on accomplishing tasks. But at times, it does mean exactly this! Yes, it could mean goal setting and developing a well-thought-out behavioral plan as a roadmap for getting from point A to point B.

Clint, a clinically depressed forty-two-year-old man, came to my office. It was clear that his desire to get out of the paralyzing funk he had endured for years was genuine. His entire body looks exhausted as Clint explains in his monotone, "Well, Dr. Castro, I really don't want to sleep all day and I tell myself the night before that tomorrow will be different. I really am convinced as I doze off to sleep that the next day will be the day I jump out of bed and go find myself a job. But it doesn't happen; I wake up and I just don't feel it. You have to believe me; I really do want to change."

My answer to Clint (in my sensitive, sweet therapist way) is, "I don't care what you *want* and I don't care how you *feel*! It is time to *do*!" For people like Clint, I will confront immediately and directly what has left them stuck for years. Clint has *wanted* to accomplish success and has *felt* his way through life for too long, and just look where it has gotten him—stuck in bed, sleeping his life away! It is time for *doing*! Yes, the time has come to push those feelings and wants to the side and jump on a step-by-step behavioral plan to accomplish the goals.

I don't try to kid Clint. "Now, Clint, when the alarm goes off tomorrow, you are not going to *want* to get out of bed or *feel* like getting out of bed. I know it and you know it. (Depression is real and it can be paralyzing.) But remember, it isn't about feeling and wanting; it is all about *doing*. So when that alarm goes off, you pick up that piece of paper on your bedside table that lists the steps to taking a shower and getting dressed.

As the story of Clint illustrates, doing something different and Giving Room to change can begin with setting specific, measurable goals and then working toward accomplishing those goals. As simple as it seems, this is exactly what some of my patients need in order to Give Themselves Room to enjoy a happier life. Their prescription is a step-by-step plan for accomplishing a specific goal, with a determined coach (me!), empowering them to follow through. The beauty of it is that it *works*, whether for a nineteen-year-old boy diagnosed with Asperger's disorder, who desperately wants a girlfriend for the first time in his life, or a thirty-eight-year-old marijuana-smoking soccer mom, who wants to give up the habit and live a healthier life with more meaningful relationships. It could even be someone as depressed as Clint, who wants a job but needs to take the first step to get out of bed. The specific goal is irrelevant. What's important—what is REALLY important—is that there is a plan and that action is taken!

Now, working to accomplish goal after goal in a driven but focused manner may not always be what this doctor orders. I may recommend just the opposite for someone obsessed with achieving success and power in life. "Venturing into the unknown" for us Rat-Racing humans (and, at times, I certainly can be one) may entail taking that to-do list and throwing it into the trash! It may be about prying yourself away from the computer on a Saturday afternoon, walking over to your child and interrupting his fourth hour of Xbox, saying, "Hey, son, I just found this old puzzle I used to do when I was eight years old! Turn off the TV. Let's do it together." As you both begin fitting the old, worn-out pieces together, you might find that life slows down and a "conversation of connection" emerges between father and son. Nothing too deep. Nothing like "What are you going to be when you're an adult?" No discussion of "Is your homework finished?" These are moments when time slowly ticks, and simple words, like puzzle pieces, fit together in a way that just "works." Lives that were disconnected are now gradually joined as the afternoon passes and a picture of understanding emerges. You are Giving Room for each other.

Giving Room is about figuring out what you need and making shifts in your life to move toward it. Painful feelings that we experience on a regular basis, such as sadness, anger, frustration, and fear, are catalysts that leave us feeling sick and tired of being sick and tired. We seek out help for a more fulfilling life. It leads us to our therapist, our minister, a yoga class, or even this book. But, like a gigantic cruise ship slowly making a left turn, change does not happen immediately. It's the subtle changes, the day-to-day changes that wake us up, maybe years later, to the knowledge in our hearts that "I have grown and I am definitely 'good enough!'" This is Giving Room for the Truth.

But what gives a person the edge to truly live life to its fullest? How does one overcome a life heavy with stress and emerge into a new life, full of confidence and possibility? When doors are shutting all around you, how do you go about Giving Room to what Buddha would call enlightenment, what Jesus would call salvation, or what rock star legend Mick Jagger would call satisfaction? Giving Room to develop that "something special" deep inside all of us that leads to a meaningful life is what this book is about. There is an old psychoanalytic term that, to me, precisely addresses the search for that elusive character trait that spurs one over the mountain and into the valley of happiness. That term is *ego strength*.

It was a rainy summer night, and my brother's black belt examination was taking place in a rickety, hundred-year-old barn house deep in the Blue Ridge Mountains. I was twelve, and my brother, Paul John, was fifteen. PJ was the youngest candidate to be competing for his black belt certification in the forty-five-year history of Sashimiti Karate Studio, which made the evening even more special. The scene felt to me like a sacred ritual of some kind, with several hundred students packed into the barn surrounding my brother. PJ sat by himself in the middle of the hardwood floor, staring straight ahead at the six instructors. Candles gently illuminated the large room. The instructors had just returned to the head table after deliberating the fate of my brother for over an hour. The moment had come. The three-hour test that had pushed my brother to his limit both physically and mentally was over. It was decision time: pass or fail.

No one else in my family was present for this monumental moment in my brother's life, just me. Everyone in the room held their breath as the tenth-degree black belt, Sensei Sashimiti, stood up to announce the verdict. The only sound was the pounding of rain on the wooden roof. The sensei spoke. "Paul Castro, please come forward."

My brother immediately sprang to his feet and jogged forward, stopping before the judges and bowing. All hearts were pounding. Sensei Sashimiti continued, "Mr. Castro, the judges have deliberated, but before we decide the results of your examination, we will need you to redo the jujitsu section [the art of several attackers coming at you, and you coming up with the many different ways to take the guys down] of the exam. Begin when you are ready."

Suddenly the room erupted into confused exclamations and cutting whispers. Everyone around me was disgustedly muttering something along the lines of: "I can't believe they're making him redo his jujitsu section! It's not fair! He's been sitting there for over an hour! He's not even warmed up anymore!"

True, it was an unusual move by the judges. Rarely will a competitor be called upon to perform again after a black belt exam has ended. The observers in the room were outraged!

I didn't feel angry or insulted for my brother. As the commotion brewed all around me, I found myself frozen in a dreamlike spell. At that moment, my world slowed down and a surreal feeling wafted through my body; as I stared at my brother, I was nearly in a trance state! Right when Sensei Sashimiti finished his words, "Begin when you are ready," my brother sprinted back to the middle of the room and immediately jumped to ready position.

As my brother methodically bounced on his toes and his attackers surrounded him, I smiled and began to cry. The odds were stacked against my brother, but I was flooded with a calming joy, because I knew something that no one else in the room knew. I knew that it was during just this kind of situation that my brother Paul is at his best! My years of growing up with him had taught me that Paul is a person who thrives when faced with a challenge. When adversity stares him in the face, he steps forward, not backward. He is a person who Gives Room to adapt and succeed throughout the constant vicissitudes of life. And he is a person with passion!

As the years have moved on, Paul and I have become closer as adults, and he still amazes me. It doesn't matter whether he's volunteering at the local Suicide Prevention Center, competing in the LA Triathlon, or cutting a high-priced movie deal with some big production studio. It is an inner strength in PJ that has allowed him to prepare so well in life and to seize opportunities when they arise, even (or especially) when faced with adversity. In psychology they call that ego strength. In religion they call it faith. I call it Giving Room.

Dr. Nancy McWilliams defines ego strength in her book *Psychoanalytic Diagnosis* as: "The person's capacity to acknowledge reality, even when it is extremely unpleasant, without resorting to more primitive defenses like denial." According to Dr. McWilliams, our fundamental task in life is to use this strength, stepping forward rather than shrinking back, when life is difficult. With unexpected curveballs constantly coming our way, only an unwavering and clear-sighted ego will Give Room for change and growth. It's about taking action and fighting the urge to bury our heads in the sand of denial, rationalization, projection, or whatever other ingenious defenses we can come up with. It is resisting the impulse to turn our backs on vulnerable feelings through unhealthy behaviors such as substance abuse and angry outbursts. It is an unflinching acknowledgment of the essential truth that "Life is difficult," or, as Gautama Buddha so succinctly put it, "Life is suffering." Of course, life is also beautiful—when you Give It Room for it to be what it is!

Dr. Martin Luther King, Mother Teresa, Gandhi, and even the modern sports icon Tiger Woods—all of these famous and inspirational people have embraced the fundamental truth that life is difficult and that Giving Room to take on its inevitable disappointments and frustrations is the key to a rewarding life. All are examples of people who understood that while change is difficult, possibility is endless. It seems to me that, sadly, most people just don't have that inner drive, that ego strength, to embrace this humbling—but magnificent—fact of life. All four of these amazing individuals entered life with the odds against them, only to knock down barriers and shift the landscape of our world for the better. All of them knew that setbacks should be welcomed. My favorite quote from Gandhi is, "Heroes are made in the hour of defeat. Success is therefore well described as a series of glorious defeats!"

Giving Room to cultivate ego strength is not an easy task. Sure, every day the scientific community tells us that genetics and biology play key roles in personality development. It is not uncommon for psychiatric disorders such as depression, schizophrenia, or ADHD to have a genetic link. For example, thirty-two-year-old Bob says during our first meeting, "My grandpa was clinically depressed and so is my father. Both have taken meds and both have been hospitalized. Personally, I can hardly get myself moving in the morning and there is this black cloud over me that never lets the sun shine through. I'm thinking I may be depressed, too." Just as with Bob, there is a biological basis to many disorders. Yet for me, when it comes to this concept known as ego strength, it's important to recognize that a person is not born with the edge. Even the best genes in the world can't automatically bestow the sense of peace and confidence that a person possesses when filled with ego strength.

As I conclude, I challenge all of you to focus on the principles described throughout this book. These principles will assist in Giving Room for change and the emergence of ego strength. The lessons I have laid out will help you find and

241

sharpen that edge. Therefore, I urge you to embrace with open arms the struggles and suffering that are at the core of living life. Let's review those life-giving principles.

1. Self-exploration and personal growth take time and patience, so keep in mind the process of de-Velcroing the mind by identifying and understanding all the "stuff" that is stuck together in our heads.

2. Step out of the Rat Race long enough to slow down and appreciate the good things in your life. Realize that you have choices and that you don't need to be captive to the rigid expectations that have been inculcated in you for years. Just like the old lessons I learned from John, my mentor in Seattle, fight valiantly NOT to get caught up in the next task on the list.

3. Commit to memory that you are unique with special talents. It's an absolute necessity to Give Yourself Room to embrace your gifts and to let it be known that you are a valuable (even precious) individual, and to focus on the positives. It is important to remember that you can change lives for the better, *even during low moments*, and do it with a smile on your face. This idea reminds me of when Mother Teresa was asked to join an angry march protesting war. She said, "I won't do it. But if you organize a pro-peace rally, I will be there." Now that's being positively proactive!

4. Stay Balanced. Too many of us fall somewhere along the extreme ends of the bell-curved narcissist-masochist

continuum. At either extreme, we are cut off from opportunities to develop true intimate relationships in life, and this leaves us lonely and resentful. Happiness is about Giving Room to move closer to the grayer areas by exposing and resisting our black-and-white thinking patterns. Generally, not seeing life in the more objective gray area of the spectrum moves us to feel unfairly wronged (masochists) or wrongly right (narcissists), and these unhealthy feelings become more severe if we do not Give Room to change. Stay balanced! When we veer toward the extreme ends of the give-take continuum, our vision of life gets cloudy; we are so myopically focused on Numero Uno that we ignore, or are blind to, the contributions of others in our relationships. We must clearly see and verbalize our role in these unhealthy relationships. By actually voicing our understanding of our place along the narcissist-masochist continuum, we Give Ourselves Room for healthier communication and stronger, long-lasting intimacy in all relationships. The key is to find the balance in the middle and to constantly be working to stay in this life-giving zone of "healthy selfishness."

5. Don't "go with your gut"! Be wary when this Rat Race world we live in constantly urges you to "go with your gut!" Like a tidal wave, the rush of our instincts can overwhelm our minds, battering us along the shores of impulsive behavior and poor judgment. Impulsively reacting to our immediate feelings can lead to regret and frustration. Giving Room to delay acting on the feeling in one's gut fosters understanding in all rela-

tionships. Because resisting this fast-moving surge of emotion can be so difficult, it is helpful to "fake or ignore" the feelings and focus solely on healthy behaviors. Pushing our minds to focus on the healthy behaviors and ignoring our thoughts and feelings is no easy task. But by doing so, our mind transcends with a clearer picture of how to proceed in a healthy way. This is how ego strength is gained and how it evolves.

6. We all need someone in our corner! Happiness in life is unattainable if you don't Give Room to let others in your corner. It is impossible for a loner to possess true ego strength. Understand that having someone throughout your life who has been there for you, *consistently*, is critical to living a contented life. These folks don't have to be perfect, just good enough. Now, if you were deprived of that caring mentor figure who would have served as a solid foundation to your psychic structure, I truly feel for you. Nevertheless, you need to trust me when I encourage you to take the scary risk of opening up and Giving Room to being vulnerable. Many of you, much like Holly, have felt that you can't trust anyone in this world, and rightly so! People have continuously let you down. But I strongly urge you to fight that fear and step forward, not backward, with a trusting heart. Healthy, trustworthy people will come into your life and they will want to be there for you. By being brave and taking this risk, your ego strength will emerge.

7. The Big P's: Parenting and Being a Partner. In my professional experience, parenting is hard; being a partner

is harder. There are many difficult jobs in life. My job list has included waiting tables, practicing psychology, teaching graduate students, selling women's handbags and gowns in a department store (maybe this is where my passion for dressing up as a woman every Halloween comes from!), delivering newspapers as a teenager, and cutting grass during summer break as a kid. Like me, I'm sure you have taken on jobs that required great effort—attorney, custodian, teacher, athlete, and so on. Some jobs pay more than others. Some jobs are more rewarding than others. But to me, the two most *difficult* and *rewarding* (with no financial gain) jobs for just about anyone in life are the two Big P's: Parent and Partner.

8. Being the perfect parent is impossible, so get that dream out of your mind immediately! At times, you are going to be inconsistent and lack empathy. Unfortunately, some of us parents, in a fit of frustration, will impulsively give our kid a smack and yell, "Stop it!" There will be moments when you will be kicking yourself for not spending enough time with your kids or failing to take a few minutes to teach them the importance of giving to others. Sadly, you will likely catch yourself herding your kids too aggressively to look to the future or you may find yourself hyperfocusing on "What are you going be when you grow up?" rather than "Who are you *right now*?" Because you are so busy running your kids around to Kumon, soccer practice, or dance class, with little time to breathe, you will forget to slow down. There will be times when you forget to create a calm,

open space for dialogue with your child about important life lessons that build much-needed frustration tolerance. You will probably forget to show them the importance of money in our society. All of us parents will screw up! Some more than others. But don't kid yourself—parenting is hard work, and perfection is unattainable.

9. Accept that you are going to make mistakes. Don't beat yourself up too much about your shortcomings as a parent. Give Room to your flaws as a caregiver. Accepting that you do and will continue to "mess up" helps keep that paralyzing guilty "critical eye" away and encourages you to refocus on the important principles you need to teach your child. For instance, remember to embrace your kids as living people with a lot to offer RIGHT NOW, *TODAY!* Try to avoid presenting your child with a checklist of goals that will presumably lead him or her to "be something" later in life. Your child is already a thriving, contributing human being! As mentioned earlier, too often the messages that advance society's push are messages of "Forward march!" rather than "Embrace the moment." We serve our children well when we let them know it's okay to Give Room to accepting what life has given them in the here and now.

10. Focus on Giving Room to being a parent who teaches and personally demonstrates the importance of giving. Not just haphazardly giving, but giving with a purpose. The act of giving makes both the giver and the receiver feel better and helps to build ego strength and tender

hearts in our young ones. It's hard to imagine the act—and the art—of giving ever being a bad thing. Yet, given the perversity of some people, even the most beautiful acts of giving can be misconstrued. For example, Oprah Winfrey recently gave forty million dollars to build an incredible educational center for impoverished girls in South Africa. The news of her generosity was on the cover of many magazines. I was appalled when I stood behind two women in the grocery store checkout aisle, flipping through one of the magazines and having a cynical discussion about Oprah's generous gift. They scoffed, "Oh, yeah, I'm sure Oprah really wanted to help those poor little girls, ha ha ha. . . . Yeah, and I bet the forty-million-dollar gift had nothing to do with generating ratings for her TV show, ha ha ha. . . ."

11. I'm a Castro, so of course I couldn't hold back. I tapped the most vocal woman on the shoulder and asked, "What if Oprah did it for several reasons?" The woman was startled and looked at me as if I had three heads. But I continued, "What if she gave the forty million because she thought it would boost her business empire? And what if she also did it in a self-serving way to get people to think, *Oh, that Oprah—she is so giving and wonderful!?* And finally, what if she also did it because she REALLY CARES, and because it has been a lifelong mission of hers to help those girls? What if it was all those things combined and not just one? If that was the case, do you think you would be standing here in line poking fun at an incredible human being who

just gave forty million dollars to children in need?" Both women just stared at me in astonishment with their mouths open.

12. The point is, *It's forty million bucks!* I mean, come on! Who cares if she wanted a little PR? What's the difference if it rakes in more cash, in the form of more profitable TV ads, for her highly successful show? The true bottom line is that Oprah is dramatically changing the lives of those very needy girls for many years to come, period! And there is absolutely nothing wrong with that! So please, don't feel guilty when your own giving is a little self-serving. It's just one aspect of the "healthy selfishness" we looked at earlier when I gave you examples (The "giving dollar" and my daughter Zoe's card-making project) of how to foster giving in kids. There are many other delightful ways to teach the art of giving, so be creative and make it a priority. When we instill giving as a priority in ourselves and in our children, ego strength grows, hearts sing, and everyone benefits.

13. Talk to your kids about money. Embracing the importance of handling money responsibly with your children imbues their early years with a respect for this medium of energetic exchange known as the almighty dollar. Sure, money can be the root of some evils. Negative emotions such as anger, jealousy, resentment, rage, fear, and so on have a way of flaring up like a brush fire when money comes into the equation. But I urge you to resist the pious tendency to vilify money. Just as I do with my daughter every Saturday morning

at the grocery store, when she stands in front of the coloring books wringing her hands, allow your kids to struggle with having to make decisions about their money. This will teach responsible spending and money management, while reducing impulsivity. By taking a proactive approach to educating your kids about the realities of money in their world, you also begin the process of helping them distinguish between what is truly a *need* and what is just a *want*.

14. Do you believe me now when I say good parenting is one of the hardest jobs out there? Parenting is not just about being told, "Oh, congratulations! You guys are such warm people and you can provide for your little one; you are going to be great parents!" Being a warm person or having a ton of money doesn't make you a great parent. The hard physical, emotional, and mental work of embracing the constant flow of changes in a child's life is what tests our mettle as parents. And the tests are never-ending! Using the age-old fundamentals of healthy parenting known as *consistency* and *follow-through* will take you a long way toward acing the tests of parenthood. Good parenting starts with clear and consistent expectations and instructions, then following through on them. I have stressed these imperatives earlier in this book to underscore the fact that good (or good enough!), consistent, follow-through parenting is tremendously hard work. It's challenging to give your kids choices that are clear, measurable, unemotional, and not too wordy. But in doing so, you will realize clarity and far greater sanity in your own

and your children's lives. This in turn will Give Kids Room for the process of building ego strength.

15. In addition to the two parenting laws of consistency and follow-through, applying appropriate discipline when our kids misbehave is essential to healthy development of ego strength. We've all seen that corporal punishment "works" in stopping a child's negative behavior, but it works like a three-day-old bandage on a skinned knee. Spanking your kid doesn't "stick" for long in teaching lasting appropriate behavior. I know at times we become so frustrated with our kids that it is so hard not to impulsively give them a smack and yell words we'll later regret. But staying away from spankings and focusing instead on the proper steps to implementing a time-out is the only way to realize lasting behavioral and attitudinal change in our children. This clear-headed restraint and determination models to our children that using *words* is the way to help people change in life, not using the "armed forces" of mindless muscles. But remember, too, if your kid comes absolutely unglued and is physically lashing out, sometimes you need to face the reality that his or her behavior is beyond your control. It's a sad and sobering possibility, but should there come a time when you can no longer handle your child, you need to be prepared to call for support, such as help from the police. While that might seem like the ultimate in draconian measures, such an act would actually be a gift that helps to teach your child right from wrong and builds their ego strength for years to come.

16. The final and MOST IMPORTANT parenting principle that I very much want you to take away from this book is: *Constantly pouncing on opportunities that build frustration tolerance in children goes a long way toward raising humble and responsible kids!* When I am counseling parents on parenting skills, I always spend time talking about building frustration tolerance in their kids. Remember the tragic narrative I offered about the Triple Whammy earlier? If your child lacks tolerance for frustration, he or she will wind up unproductive, depressed, and bitter at the world for "turning its back" on him or her. Your kids need the guidance and strength from you, their mentors, to not shy away from situations that may be uncomfortable, embarrassing, or generally difficult for them. Considering the Premack principle and natural consequences, we can look at the frustrating situations our kids face as real opportunities to build tolerance for the inevitable struggles in life. This is Giving Room for healthy child development, and it ultimately encourages the emergence of ego strength in our young ones.

17. Just as there are principles that Give Kids Room to find fulfillment and joy in their lives, so, too, are there guidelines that lead to success in that other exceptionally difficult and rewarding job: being someone's loving partner. There are three musts when Giving Room for healthy growth in your intimate relationships. You must put in the time, work at the relationship, and take the risk of putting yourself in a vulnerable position. In other words, your intimate relationship needs to be

your top priority. Also, you would serve your relationship well to slow down and look deeply into your partner's eyes, where you will find not only a soul but a human being with very specific needs. Indeed, taking the time to "connect with your eyes" is one of the most intimate of all connections you can experience with your loved one. It brings understanding and compassion. So make it a priority to look into your partner's eyes more often!

18. Responding to a loved one's needs, or at least honestly letting that person know you are not willing or able to attend to their needs, Gives Room for growth. Responding to your partner's needs may mean lending a caring ear—inviting him or her to describe and elaborate on their most intimate and vulnerable feelings. By giving a caring ear, you are providing an invaluable gift while also avoiding the contamination of emotional moments with words! What better way to foster intimacy and give birth to a satisfying relationship! Bear in mind, it is so important to see your marriage as occupying the very top tier of your "hierarchy of life," with you and your partner holding hands there, side by side. Every other priority—your job, your hobbies, your pets, your vacations, and, yes, even your kids, should all trickle down from there. It all comes together at the top—your relationship, perfectly poised atop a strong foundation of family solidarity.

Holly's story, although traumatic and dramatic, is in many ways no different from yours or mine. We have all run across hardships in our world, some more than others. Maybe you have endured the death of a loved one. Perhaps you were sexually abused as a child. It could be that you have struggled with a physical disease or limitation for many years. Or, possibly, your mother, like Holly's, wasn't even a good-enough mother. No matter what trials and tribulations you have met along your way, pat yourself on the back FIRST for taking a beneficial step by reading this book. You were in some kind of emotional pain, and good for you for Giving Yourself Room to explore the principles I have outlined! I hope it is a starting point for continued emotional growth.

But don't stop now! Apply these lessons to your everyday life. Courageously accept that life is difficult and don't expect change to come overnight. Sure, people do change; I see it every day in my office. But the world can rattle our resolve and beckon us to join the Rat Race, making our days so darn challenging. To stay on course, be sure that the ugly stumbling block called guilt is cleared from your path or nimbly sidestepped. Give Room to de-Velcro your mind and see life on a more neutral gray continuum, not in black and white. Allow your gut to communicate with you, but be on guard against impulsively reacting to those feelings deep inside. And finally, invite others to be in your corner. Lean on them. Let them lean on you! Open your arms to them. And embrace their giving nature with confidence and trust.

Parents, remember to focus on building your child's frustration tolerance through healthy forms of discipline—not just giving your kid a smack or a reprimand every time you are annoyed. They may not like you now, but as they mature into ethical and humble adults with an ample supply of frustration tolerance, they will thank you and respect you. Concentrate on

253

providing consistency and follow-through in your child's life through the Premack principle and by stressing natural consequences. Step forward to teach your kid about the realities of money and the importance and rewards of giving. Open your heart and listen to others with a caring ear. As for your intimate relationship, Give Room to your partner, encouraging that special person to express his or her needs. Then, work to sensitively respond to those needs with great passion and conviction. By making your intimate relationship *the* priority in your life, you map a healthy path to fulfillment.

You have Given Yourself Room to learn about Giving Room. I congratulate you! Now continue along that unknown, scary road of change. There is a light at the end of this tunnel. That light is your ego strength, and I know it will show you the way.

SUGGESTED READING

Brent J. Atkinson, *Emotional Intelligence in Couples Therapy: Advances from Neurobiology and the Science of Intimate Relationships* (New York: W. W. Norton, 2005).

Susan M. Johnson, *The Practice of Emotionally Focused Couple Therapy: Creating Connection* (New York: Brunner-Routledge, 2004).

Meg Meeker, *Strong Fathers, Strong Daughters: 10 Secrets Every Father Should Know* (Washington, DC: Regnery, 2006).

M. Scott Peck, *The Road Less Traveled* (New York: Simon & Schuster, 1985).

Dave Pelzer, *A Child Called "It": One Child's Courage to Survive* (Deerfield Beach, FL: Health Communications, 1997).

———, *The Lost Boy: A Foster Child's Search for the Love of a Family* (Deerfield Beach, FL: Health Communications, 1997).

David Shapiro, *Neurotic Styles* (New York: Basic Books, 1965).

Abigail Thomas, *A Three Dog Life* (Orlando, FL: Harcourt, 2006).

Jeannette Walls, *The Glass Castle: A Memoir* (New York: Scribner, 2005).

SUGGESTED READING

Daniel B. Wile, *Couples Therapy: A Nontraditional Approach* (New York: Wiley, 1993).

Irvin D. Yalom, *Love's Executioner and Other Tales of Psychotherapy* (New York: Basic Books, 1989).

Michael D. Yapko, *Breaking the Patterns of Depression* (New York: Doubleday, 1997).

BIBLIOGRAPHY

Freud, Anna. *The Ego and the Mechanisms of Defense.* Rev. ed. Madison, CT: International Universities Press, 1996.

McWilliams, Nancy. *Psychoanalytic Diagnosis: Understanding Personality Structure in the Clinical Process.* New York: Guilford Press, 1994.

Mogel, Wendy. *The Blessing of a Skinned Knee: Using Jewish Teachings to Raise Self-Reliant Children.* New York: Penguin Group, 2001.

Moore, Burness, and Bernard Fine, eds. *Psychoanalytic Terms and Concepts.* New Haven, CT, and London: American Psychoanalytic Association and Yale University Press, 1990.

INDEX

INDEX

261

INDEX

INDEX

ABOUT THE AUTHOR

photo by Mindy Blives McCoy

Aᴺᴛʜᴏɴʏ J. Cᴀsᴛʀᴏ, PʜD, is a clinical psychologist who treats young children, adolescents, adults, and couples. An expert in the field of adult and child psychology, Dr. Castro frequently speaks before audiences of parents, colleagues, and teachers in the St. Louis community.